2nd edition

CB135016

masterMind

Student's Book

Mickey Rogers
Steve Taylore-Knowles
Dorothy E. Zemach

Concept development:
Mariela Gil Vierma

Level 2a

MACMILLAN

Contents

PRONUNCIATION	GRAMMAR	VOCABULARY	LIFESKILLS
WORDS: intonation and attitude	**ADVERB PHRASES** FUNCTION giving additional information **NEGATIVE QUESTIONS** FUNCTION confirming an existing belief	**CONSUMERISM AND SUSTAINABILITY** FUNCTION discussing ways to reduce consumption **DESCRIBING USED ITEMS** FUNCTION posting ads on a website	**SELF & SOCIETY:** Building communities FUNCTION creating a new community
	LANGUAGE WRAP-UP		
WORDS: contrastive stress	**FUTURE PASSIVE** FUNCTION talking about inventions of the future **CONDITIONAL CONJUNCTIONS** FUNCTION talking about space programs of the future	**BUSINESS AND INNOVATION** FUNCTION talking about how companies launch innovations **NEGATIVE PREFIXES *UN-*, *IM-*, *IN-*** FUNCTION talking about space exploration	**STUDY & LEARNING:** Evaluating explanations FUNCTION distinguishing between correlation and causation
	LANGUAGE WRAP-UP		
WORDS: connected speech—final consonant sound to first vowel sound	**OBJECT COMPLEMENTS** FUNCTION talking about data security **NEGATIVE STRUCTURES WITH *THINK*, *SUPPOSE*, ETC.** FUNCTION giving opinions on online privacy	**DIGITAL PRIVACY** FUNCTION talking about online privacy issues **PHRASAL VERBS** FUNCTION talking about identity theft	**SELF & SOCIETY:** **PROTECTING DIGITAL PRIVACY** FUNCTION giving advice
	LANGUAGE WRAP-UP		
SOUNDS: vowel length before final consonant sounds	**RELATIVE PRONOUNS WITH *–EVER*** FUNCTION talking about online study **MIXED CONDITIONALS** FUNCTION talking about hypothetical situations in education	**VERB COLLOCATIONS** FUNCTION talking about higher education **WORDS RELATED TO STAND** FUNCTION talking about the job market	**SELF & SOCIETY:** **ANTICIPATING CULTURAL DIFFERENCES** FUNCTION finding information needed in advance
	LANGUAGE WRAP-UP		
SOUNDS: final consonant clusters	**IMPERSONAL PASSIVE** FUNCTION talking about beliefs **PASSIVE MODALS** FUNCTION giving opinions on wildlife issues	**ANIMAL RESCUE** FUNCTION talking about wildlife conservation **ADVERB-ADJECTIVE COLLOCATIONS** FUNCTION talking about wildlife population issues	**SELF & SOCIETY:** **UNDERSTANDING DECISION-MAKING STYLES** FUNCTION making decisions as a group
	LANGUAGE WRAP-UP		
SOUNDS: linking words with a /w/ or a /j/ sound	**FUTURE PERFECT** FUNCTION making predictions for specific times in the future **FUTURE PERFECT PROGRESSIVE** FUNCTION predicting ongoing events at specific times in the future	**PHRASES WITH ADJECTIVE + PREPOSITION** FUNCTION talking about automation in vehicles **PHRASAL VERBS** FUNCTION talking about robots in the workplace	**STUDY & LEARNING:** **ORGANIZING AN ARGUMENT** FUNCTION selecting and organizing points to make
	LANGUAGE WRAP-UP		

Grammar review

1 Circle the mistake in each sentence and correct it.

1 My friends would always telling me to go out more. ______
2 Ian is used to speak French. He's lived in Montreal for two years. ______
3 Emma is always get lost on campus. She needs a map. ______
4 I never used drink bottled water until recently. ______
5 My aunt's and uncle's favorite hotel was designed by a rock star. ______

2 Complete the sentences with the modal verbs from the box. You can use some words more than once, and there may be more than one correct answer.

must can't could might may

1 I'm not sure why they aren't here yet. Their car ______ have broken down, I suppose.
2 Did you hear all the people celebrating at the stadium? Their team ______ have won the game.
3 I haven't seen James at work for a few weeks. Do you think he ______ have quit?
4 Where's Patty? She was here a minute ago. She ______ have vanished!
5 Check your missed calls! She ______ have called while you were in a meeting. You never know.

3 Choose the correct verb tense.

1 In the future, people in low-lying countries *may be living* / *are living* in floating houses.
2 Luckily, we *had taken* / *had been taking* several photographs of the view before it clouded over.
3 We hope that by this time next year, a new government *is going to run* / *will be running* the country.
4 By the time Alex arrived, his colleagues *had been discussing* / *had discussed* the proposal for over an hour.
5 Many customers' online accounts *have been* / *are being* hacked recently.

4 Complete the story using the correct form of the verbs in parentheses.

I **(1)** ______ (*have*) an interesting time on my date at the restaurant. We had just finished our main course and Eva **(2)** ______ (*tell*) me about her driving test. Luckily she **(3)** ______ (*pass*), so the small mistake she made when she couldn't turn off the windshield wipers **(4)** ______ (*seem*) pretty funny. Then, in the middle of her story she **(5)** ______ (*stop*) and said she had to leave. I was left alone to pay the bill, and that's when I realized I **(6)** ______ (*leave*) my wallet at home.

5 Rewrite the direct speech as reported speech in two different ways (with and without backshifting) where possible. Use the verbs in parentheses.

1 "I hadn't sent the email when you asked me about it yesterday." (*admit*)
My colleague ______.
2 "Most of the original Native American languages no longer exist." (*declare*)
A researcher ______.
3 "The winner of the *X Factor* has gotten his first number-one hit." (*report*)
MusicReview.com ______.
4 "Usain Bolt will not take part in this year's Indoor Athletic Championships." (*announce*)
Usain Bolt's trainer ______.
5 "I'll send you a text in ten minutes." (*said*)
An hour ago, Nick ______, but he never did.

6 Choose the correct verb form.

1 We regret *informing* / *to inform* you that your application will not be taken further.
2 We tried *liking* / *to like* chili while we were in Mexico, but we just couldn't. It was too spicy!
3 He always complains about *washing* / *to wash* the dishes.
4 Everyone is looking forward to *meeting* / *meet* the new student in the class.
5 Did someone forget *mailing* / *to mail* this letter? Look! It's still on my desk.

7 Complete the sentences with the words from the box. Some can be used more than once.

for   so as to   so that   to

1 Employees should check their emails at the same time every day __________ manage their time better.
2 We joined a social networking site __________ keep in touch with old friends.
3 We booked our tickets well in advance __________ avoid paying a higher price.
4 We are building wells in rural areas __________ local residents can drink safe, clean water.
5 For his birthday, I bought Larry a mug __________ drinking his coffee in the morning.

8 Complete the text using the correct form of *get/be used to* and the verbs in parentheses.

My name's Adriana, and I just left high school and started a job as an air stewardess. I **(1)** *'m not used to working* (*not work*) these kinds of shifts and I find it really difficult to get up at 3 a.m. And I really have to **(2)** __________ (*speak*) English all the time—sometimes I forget and the passengers don't understand me! I **(3)** __________ (*listen*) to English—on TV, for example—but I **(4)** __________ (*not speak*) English outside of school. It's nice earning money, though. I **(5)** __________ (*not pick up*) a paycheck each week—I still get excited about it! The uniform isn't bad. I **(6)** __________ (*wear*) the same thing every day. At least I save money on new clothes.

9 Complete the conditional sentences with the correct form of the verb in parentheses.

1 If you had a sense of humor, you __________ (*see*) the funny side of the joke.
2 I wouldn't try the spicy dishes if I __________ (*be*) you.
3 Some traditions wouldn't have been lost if the languages they belonged to __________ (*survive*).
4 If you __________ (*use*) a firewall, you won't be bombarded with emails from unknown senders.
5 If you change your diet, you __________ (*reduce*) your calorie intake.
6 If you hadn't shopped at the large supermarkets, you __________ (*boost*) the local economy.

10 Rewrite the sentences using the prompts and the words in parentheses.

1 A volunteer succeeded in raising $500 for a charity that helps the homeless. (*manage to*)
A volunteer __________.
2 I'm afraid parents can't park outside the school if they don't have a permit. (*allow*)
Parents are __________.
3 My colleague said, "If I were you, I wouldn't drive to work in these floods." (*warn*)
We were __________.
4 Although Sophie enjoys designing clothes, she doesn't want to organize a fashion show. (*despite*)
Sophie __________.
5 Greater numbers of people are living together before getting married. (*more and more*)
A study reported that __________.

11 Complete the noun clauses with *why*, *what*, *where*, *when*, or *how*.

1 You can see __________ a lot of celebrities don't enjoy the spotlight.
2 I'm not sure __________ that movie is on. Check in the TV listings page.
3 They told me __________ I could attend a meeting about volunteering: at City Hall.
4 Do you know __________ the Hindu calendar celebrates in autumn?
5 Newspapers are learning __________ to adapt to the changing world of technology.

12 In each sentence, two connectors are correct. Cross out the *incorrect* connector.

1 People campaign for causes they believe in. *Besides that, / Despite the fact, / Moreover,* they want to inform and help others.
2 The internet has made communication easier. *Moreover, / Furthermore, / However,* people have learned more about other cultures.
3 Local farmers can stay in business *as a result of / in spite of / due to* people buying their products.
4 Many people do extreme sports *in spite of the fact that / despite / even though* they are aware of the risks involved.
5 This area of coastline was hit by a hurricane last month. *However, / Therefore, / Nevertheless,* few buildings were destroyed.

UNIT 1 MONEY-FREE

IN THIS UNIT YOU

- learn language to talk about consumerism and sustainable living
- read about someone's experiment in living without money
- talk about giving things away for free
- listen to a radio interview about bartering
- write ads for second-hand items
- learn about building different kinds of communities
- watch a video about growing sustainable food

READING
text organization

Is text organization important? What makes a reading text well organized?

SPEAKING
hedging

We often try not to present our opinions too forcefully or too directly. Do you know any phrases we use to do that?

LIFE SKILLS
SELF & SOCIETY

building communities One community or social group you may belong to is your English class. What other communities do you belong to?

A Work in pairs. Decide what each of the pictures says about money or the lack of money.

A: *I think the first photo shows how we don't need money for everything. There are lots of things we can make or grow ourselves.*

B: *I agree. And it's more sustainable that way, too.*

1

2

3

4

B Work in pairs. Imagine each picture is from an advertising campaign. Decide what you think each picture might be used to advertise. Write a short advertising caption to accompany each picture.

1 READING: text organization

Understanding how a text is organized can help with comprehension. A key part of text organization is the way different parts of a text relate to each other. Within a paragraph, we can usually see a logical continuation of a topic from one sentence to another. Sometimes the connection between sentences is signaled by linking expressions such as *therefore* and *however,* but often we have to look for other clues. If you don't understand something in one sentence, it is helpful to look at the sentences immediately before and after it, as the ideas will usually be connected.

A Read the online feature article. Who is Mark? What reasons does he give for his experiment in living without money?

A free life is rich

Mark Boyle, a "freeconomist," gave up cash for more than two years while living in a trailer.

[1]I gave up money for two-and-a-half years and I've never been happier and healthier. To prepare, I wrote down everything I consumed, and the list was embarrassingly long. I did it because I wanted to reconnect directly with the things I use. In my view, the key reason for so many problems in the world today, such as ecological destruction, sweatshops, and factory farming, is the fact that we no longer have to see the direct repercussions of our actions. **(1)** __

[2]To start my moneyless life, I got a trailer that somebody didn't want anymore. I also decided to volunteer at an organic farm, and in return they allowed me to park my new home in an orchard. **(2)** __ When I went for a walk, I would go foraging for food. Cooking was on a camping stove outside. I bathed in a river, and my toothpaste was made from washed-up cuttlefish bones and fennel seeds. **(3)** __ Washing clothes was probably the only drag. Between making the detergent from a plant called soapwort and hand-washing the clothes, it took much longer.

[3]To get around I had a bike and trailer, and the 36-mile round-trip to the city on my bike acted as my gym membership. I grew almost all my own food and, depending on the season, I would supplement it with a bit of foraged food and on rare occasions, some bartering or looking in dumpsters. The most common item you find in dumpsters is bread because it's not homemade anymore. If you make your own bread, you don't waste a crumb. **(4)** __

[4]I had a normal upbringing. We didn't have lots of money, but I had everything I needed. After studying business and economics, I spent five years managing organic food companies. I thought this was creating a good livelihood, but I realized ethical business would never be quite enough.

[5]The response to my experiments has been mixed. **(5)** __ It's up to the individual to interpret what I'm doing any way they want. The way we live now is so inherently unsustainable that I think it will have to change at some point. What I'm trying to do is explore what could come next, that's all.

[6]Could we all live moneyless tomorrow? Of course not. Our culture is addicted to money. What we can do, however, is to start making a transition to a way of living where we're less dependent on money. If you want to go moneyless—or use less money—you need to look at your life and decide whether you want to reestablish real relationships, either with your environment or community.

www.thesundaytimes.co.uk

B **Read the text again. Write the letter of each sentence (a–e) in the correct blank (1–5).**

a) I take my fair share of abuse, but that's fine.
b) I used beeswax candles for lighting.
c) The one thing I did buy was a solar panel because I needed a way to fuel my laptop to write my first book, *The Moneyless Man*, and to communicate my experiment to the world.
d) If you pick up a loaf cheaply at the supermarket, you don't care if it goes out of date because it doesn't have any real value to you.
e) The degree of separation between the consumer and the consumed has increasingly widened, to the point that we are now completely unaware of the problems caused in the production of the food and other "stuff" we buy.

C **Work in pairs. Decide what exactly gave you the answers in Exercise B. Consider the topic, the vocabulary used, and any other aspect of the language.**

D **VOCABULARY: CONSUMERISM AND SUSTAINABILITY** **Match the words and phrases (1–8) with the definitions (a–h).**

1	consume	a)	to search in a wide area for something, especially food
2	sweatshop	b)	to use a supply of something such as time, energy, or fuel
3	factory farming	c)	a large metal container used in the building industry for waste
4	forage	d)	an intensive form of agriculture where animals have little space
5	barter	e)	(not) capable of continuing for a long time without harming the environment
6	dumpster	f)	to exchange goods/services for other goods/services instead of using money
7	livelihood	g)	something such as your work that provides the money that you need to live
8	(un)sustainable	h)	a factory where the people very work hard in bad conditions and earn very little

E **VOCABULARY: CONSUMERISM AND SUSTAINABILITY** **Work in groups. Discuss the questions.**

1 Do you think people consume too much these days? Are most people's lifestyles sustainable? Why or why not?
2 Do you think a system of bartering could work in your community? Or, would it threaten some people's livelihoods?
3 If you were taking part in an experiment in living without money, would you prefer to forage for naturally-growing food, or look in dumpsters for food people have thrown away? Which method would be more successful?
4 In both sweatshops and factory farms, goods are produced using intensive methods, and people or animals suffer. Why does this happen, and do you think it is justified? What, if anything, should be done about it?

2 PRONUNCIATION: intonation and attitude

A **1.01** **Listen to the sentence read in three different ways. Notice the different forms of intonation used.**

You're really good at saving money.

B **1.02** **Listen to and practice each sentence read in doubtful, surprised, and sarcastic ways. Then work in pairs. Choose one way to say each one. Your partner guesses which attitude you are showing.**

1 Freecycling sounds like a great idea.
2 You can find interesting things in dumpsters.

3 GRAMMAR: adverb phrases

A LANGUAGE IN CONTEXT Read the excerpt from an article. What is the purpose of Freecycle?

Waste Not, Want Not

Looking for a coffee maker or a spare tire? Want to get rid of a dog collar or some used clothes? Last week, all of these items appeared on Freecycle. Freecycle.org is an online nonprofit group that is used by many people every day. The concept is wonderfully simple! People use the website to give away and get things in their local communities. By distributing items to people who want them, Freecycle keeps "junk" out of landfills. From time to time, people ask for items that they think someone else might not want. This keeps them from making unnecessary purchases. Both requested and offered items are always free.

The organization was founded in 2003 by Deron Beal in Tucson, Arizona. He created it to help both people and the environment. The group is a worldwide network that is growing by the day. Join Freecycle by signing up online—of course, it is free to join! Local networks are moderated by volunteers.

NOTICE!

In the third sentence, which phrase tells you when something happened? In the second from last sentence, which phrase tells you how to do something?

B ANALYZE Read the excerpt in Exercise A again.

Form Complete the table with examples from the text.

Type of adverb	Adverb phrases in sentences
Time	(1) ________, all of these items appeared on Freecycle.
Frequency	Freecycle.org is a group that is used by many people (2) ________.
Place	Freecycle keeps "junk" (3) ________.
Manner	(4) ________, Freecycle keeps "junk" out of landfills. Join Freecycle (5) ________.
Purpose	People use the website (6) ________.

Function Complete the explanation with the words from the box.

how   how often   when   where   why

Adverb phrases are groups of words in a sentence that perform the same function as adverbs. They can describe time (answering the question "(1) ________?"), frequency ("(2) ________?"), place ("(3) ________?"), manner ("(4) ________?"), and purpose ("(5) ________?").

C PRACTICE Next to each of the adverb phrases, write *how*, *how often*, *when*, *where*, or *why*. Then complete each sentence with the letter of the correct adverb phrase.

a) at their convenience ________   b) by giving your unwanted item away ________
c) every now and then ________   d) for free ________
e) for space reasons ________   f) in their closets ________

Why would someone give away a new item (1) ____? Well, it may be (2) ____. (3) ____, people want to clean out their houses. They probably have items (4) ____ they don't wear. Plus, it's so easy to post an offer online and have someone come pick up the item (5) ____. Also, (6) ____, you can feel good about helping another person.

D NOW YOU DO IT Work in groups. Discuss the questions.

1 Think of some items that you would like to get rid of. When and where did you get them? Why don't you want them anymore?
2 How do you usually get rid of things you don't want? Are there other ways to get rid of things?

4 WRITING: *offer* and *wanted* ads

A Work in pairs. Read the Freecycle posts. Then talk with your partner. Which of the items offered would you want?

WANTED Second-hand dresser for college student. Condition doesn't matter. I don't have a car, so I'd appreciate it if you could drop it off.

OFFER Several stuffed animals up for grabs. As an added incentive, I'll throw in a basket to keep them in. Email me if you'd like to see some pictures.

OFFER DVD player in good working order. I don't need it because I bought another one. You must be able to pick it up before the weekend.

B VOCABULARY: DESCRIBING USED ITEMS Write an underlined word or phrase from Exercise A next to each definition.

1 ______________________: used previously; not new
2 ______________________: deliver it
3 ______________________: the physical state of something
4 ______________________: available; being offered for free
5 ______________________: able to be used successfully; not broken
6 ______________________: add to something for no additional charge

C VOCABULARY: DESCRIBING USED ITEMS Look back at Exercise A. Write two *offer* posts to appear on a freecycling website. Describe the items you have that you'd like to give away. Write two *wanted* posts about items you'd like to get from someone else. Use words and phrases from Exercise B. Then share your posts with the class.

5 SPEAKING: hedging

When we make a statement, we often use phrases that make the statement less forceful or which make it clear that this is a personal opinion, and there is room for disagreement. This is known as hedging. We do this to be polite and to show that we respect any differences of opinion.

A 1.03 Listen to six people expressing their opinions on freecycling websites as part of a college campus survey. For each person, write a hedging word or short phrase he or she uses.

1 … they're ______________________ a waste of time.
2 I'm ______________________ a site like that …
3 … it ______________________ not everyone is on there for the right reasons.
4 … but ______________________ they're generally a good thing.
5 ______________________ they're one of the most useful things on the internet.
6 … and I ______________________ they might do some good.

B Work in pairs. Discuss the questions. Use hedging phrases to make your opinion less forceful.

1 Would you use a freecycling website? If so, what for?
2 Do you think we consume too much? If so, how could we consume less?

6 GRAMMAR: negative questions

A 1.04 **LANGUAGE IN CONTEXT** **Listen to the conversation. How did Eric get his new jacket?**

Matt: Hey, Eric! Isn't that a new jacket? Where'd you get it?
Eric: Didn't I tell you? I joined a bartering website and got it there.
Matt: No, you didn't tell me. A bartering website? What's that?
Eric: It's where you trade goods and services you have for goods and services you want. Haven't you heard of them? I'm surprised. They're really popular.
Matt: Isn't it just a way for people to get rid of old stuff?
Eric: No, not at all! Mostly it's about new things and services. For example, didn't you say you want to learn to play the guitar?
Matt: Yes, but I can't afford lessons.
Eric: Right. So think of something you can do, like washing cars, or mowing someone's lawn. You put a listing on the website, and maybe someone who can play guitar will give you lessons in exchange for washing their car.
Matt: Sounds interesting! Give me the address, and I'll check it out.
Eric: Sure. I'll send you the link.

NOTICE!

What is the first question Matt asks?
What makes this a negative question?

B **ANALYZE** **Read the conversation in Exercise A again.**

Form **Complete the table with examples from the text. Then find and underline further examples in the text.**

auxiliary verb + *n't* + subject	(1) ________ tell you?
	(2) ________ heard of them?
	(3) ________ just a way ...?

Function **Choose the correct options to complete the explanation.**

A negative question can be used to confirm a belief.
Isn't that a new jacket? I haven't seen it before.
Here the speaker expects the answer to be (1) *Yes, it is.* / *No, it isn't.*

A negative question can also be used to show that we are surprised by something.
Haven't you heard of this band? They're really famous!
Here the speaker is surprised that his friend (2) *has* / *hasn't* heard of this band.

A negative question can also be used to express an opinion or make a suggestion in a (3) *more* / *less* forceful way, inviting the other person to (4) *agree* / *disagree* with us.
Isn't this a beautiful dress? *Yes, it is!*
Shouldn't you tell him? *Yes, I suppose I should.*

C **PRACTICE** **Write negative questions to complete the conversations using the words and phrases in parentheses.**

1 A: ________________________? (*be / new hat*)
B: Yes! Do you like it?
2 A: ________________________? (*find / anything interesting on the site*)
B: No, I didn't. Nobody had anything I wanted.
3 A: ________________________? (*offer / services as a mechanic*)
B: Well, I could, but that's too much like my day job!
4 A: ________________________?
(*bartering / become more common in the future?*)
B: Oh, it definitely will! It'll be used for a lot of things

WATCH OUT!

✓ A: Isn't it a bit too expensive?
B: Yes, it is.
✗ A: Isn't it a bit too expensive?
B: Yes, it's.

D **NOW YOU DO IT** **Work in pairs. Role-play a conversation where you discuss what you could possibly offer on a bartering website. Use negative questions where appropriate.**

A: *Couldn't we wash people's cars?*
B: *Yes, I guess we could. Isn't there something more interesting we could do?*

7 LISTENING: to a radio interview

A Work in pairs. Look at the pictures. Discuss the questions.

a haircut

mowing the lawn

two tennis rackets

cook and serve dinner for four

1 What would you expect to pay for each item or service?
2 What do you own, or what can you do, that you think someone would trade each item or service for?

B 1.05 Listen to the radio interview. Number the topics in the order you hear them.

a) The cost to participants ☐
b) What the organization is and how it works ☐
c) How bartering creates a community ☐
d) How businesses benefit from bartering ☐
e) The types of items and services that people barter ☐

C Listen again and correct the mistake in each sentence.

1 Bartering as a system is probably as old as selling things.
2 *Barterrific* bartered real estate for television commercials.
3 About 14% of the bartering is for services.
4 Jim Rockgate says that hotels have a small mark-up for their room rates.
5 Monetary systems relieve pressure and emotional stress.

D Work in groups. Discuss the questions.

1 What are some advantages of bartering over buying and selling? What are some disadvantages?
2 Are there any types of goods or services that you think could not (or should not) be bartered? If so, what types, and why?
3 Do you think bartering will become more or less common in the future? Why?

lifeSkills

BUILDING COMMUNITIES

- Consider the type of community you wish to create.
- Decide on the community's goals and how they will be organized.
- Advertise your community so interested people can join.

A **Work in pairs. Read the descriptions of four different types of communities. Then answer the questions.**

community /kəˈmjunəti/ ***(n.)***
the people who live in an area; a group of people in a larger society who are the same in some way

1 What specific examples of each type of community can you name?
2 Do you belong, or have you ever belonged, to any similar communities? Which ones?

A Hobby clubs / School clubs

People with a shared interest in a wide variety of sports and other activities, from singing to science to volunteer work, meet to practice or share ideas.

B Social, political, or religious groups

People in a larger community such as a city or town who have similar beliefs and values hold meetings to discuss experiences, make plans, give and receive information, or take actions.

C Online social networking sites

Sites such as Facebook and LinkedIn encourage friends and family members to share news, thoughts, pictures, videos, and web links with each other. People sometimes connect with new acquaintances by adding the friends of their friends to their networks.

D Online forums

People come together online to discuss something they are interested in, to swap questions and answers on their area of interest, and to chat socially with fellow enthusiasts.

B **Work in pairs. Match the statements with the descriptions in Exercise A. Each statement may apply to more than one description.**

1 Members see each other in person regularly.
2 Communication is probably daily or several times a week.
3 Members have a specific goal.
4 Members could become close friends.
5 It's possible that members would never see each other.
6 Members often belong to the same family.
7 Members help each other with problems and difficulties.
8 There is often a fee for joining the group.

Self and Society
Work and Career
Study and Learning

C Look at the webpage and say what kind of community the organizers of Service Swap are trying to build. Then complete the webpage with the words and phrases from the blue box.

Community statement	Expenses and fundraising	How it works	Name of community	Potential members

LIFTOFF: the crowdfunding website

LIFTOFF *is a website that is designed to help you get your project off the ground, whether it's an online social network for your neighborhood, a club of people with a common interest, or a product you want to bring to market! Tell us about your project and start attracting support today!*

(1) ______________________: Service Swap

(2) ______________________: Service Swap is a community of like-minded people who wish to use their skills and knowledge to escape the unnecessary pressure that money puts on all of us. We believe that we all have something to trade, from washing cars and mowing lawns to teaching piano and styling hair. By exchanging our services in a fair way, we believe that we can come together as a community, while also saving money in the process!

(3) ______________________: Due to the nature of swapping services, members must live within 30 miles of downtown Tampa. For most services, members need to be able to meet up in order to provide or receive their chosen service. We may make an exception for members who wish to offer and receive online services only (e.g., translation).

(4) ______________________: Service Swap members will advertise their services on the community webpage. Members will assign a monetary value for their entire service or an hour of their service to help members decide on fair trades. However, all swaps must be completely non-monetary! Membership in the group is also free of charge. Each member must offer at least one service in order to be eligible to trade for other services. Members may offer as many services as they like.

(5) ______________________: Membership is totally free and always will be. We are looking for funding to help us set the project up and to cover incidental expenses, such as webhosting. We are planning to host occasional fundraising events in our local area, which will fund the project once initial funding runs out, and will also provide excellent opportunities for members to get to know each other. These events could include yard sales and coffee mornings.

D Work in small groups. Decide on a type of community to create. Then design a webpage to advertise your community on LIFTOFF. Use the example in Exercise C as a model. Try to make your community sound as attractive to potential members as possible.

E Present your ideas to the class. Try to interest your classmates in joining your community.

F Discuss the questions.

1 What have you learned about building communities?
2 What kinds of community would you like to be involved in building in the future?

REFLECT ... How can the skill of building communities be useful to you in **Work & Career** and **Study & Learning**?

RESEARCH ...

Find out about an unusual community (a community of artists, an unusual club, etc.). Find out how it was created and how it developed. Make brief notes and report back on what you found.

Language wrap-up

1 VOCABULARY

A Complete the paragraph with the correct form of the words from the box. One word is not used. (5 points)

barter consume forage livelihood sweatshop unsustainable

Many people believe that the way we are living today is **(1)** ________________, with people **(2)** ________________ resources at a rate the planet cannot bear for long. They point to **(3)** ________________, where people work long hours for little pay. These, they say, are the inevitable consequences of a drive to make a profit at all costs. On the other hand, many people's **(4)** ________________ depend on the economy as it stands, and alternative economic models, such as ones where people **(5)** ________________ products and services, seem to be small-scale experiments that make no real difference.

B Complete the text with the words and phrases from the box. (5 points)

condition drop them off in good working order second-hand up for grabs

(1) ________________ ITEMS OFFERED: Small refrigerator, a few years old, but still **(2)** ________________. Also **(3)** ________________ is a TV in excellent **(4)** ________________. I need to get rid of these items as soon as possible, so as an added incentive I will **(5)** ________________ for you.

8–10 correct: I can talk about consumerism and sustainability and describe used items.
0–7 correct: Look again at Sections 1 and 4 on pages 10, 11, and 13. **SCORE:** /10

2 GRAMMAR

A Put the words in the correct order to form sentences with adverb phrases. Add commas and any other words that are necessary. (5 points)

1 to shoppers / more stores / recent times / have started / offer "free" items / .

____

2 to come / real purpose / is to get shoppers / the store / .

____

3 other things / the shoppers / once they are inside / spend their money / .

____

4 the free item / in this way / an incentive / becomes / .

____

5 this tactic / who visit stores / those of us / a daily basis / know / .

____

B Complete the negative questions using the verbs in parentheses. Add any other words that are necessary. (5 points)

A: **(1)** ________________ (*be*) a beautiful day? I'm looking forward to our trip this weekend.
B: Yes, the weather's great, but **(2)** ________________ (*tell*) you the trip was canceled?
A: Oh, no, you didn't. **(3)** ________________ (*be*) the booking confirmed?
B: Well, it was, but then Tom dropped out. **(4)** ________________ (*know*) he was ill?
A: Yes, I did know that, but **(5)** ________________ (*say*) he was better?
B: I did, and he was, but he's in the hospital again so we had to cancel the trip.

8–10 correct: I can place adverb phrases in a sentence and use negative questions.
0–7 correct: Look again at Sections 3 and 6 on pages 12 and 14. **SCORE:** /10

WRITING WORKSHOP Writing a proposal

A **Read the proposal. How does the writer plan to make the improvements without spending a large amount of money?**

PROPOSAL REGARDING THE STUDENT UNION BUILDING IMPROVEMENTS

FAO: George Anderson, Building Manager

Introduction
The student union building was last improved five years ago. Recently, it has become apparent that further improvements are required, with a small budget being available. After speaking to users of the building, I would like to offer the following suggestions.

Seating
It seems that the plastic furniture in social areas of the building is unpopular. Users report that it is uncomfortable, as well as unattractive. New furniture would be too costly. A much more affordable option I would like to put forward is acquiring second-hand furniture through freecycling websites. On these websites, people offer unwanted goods, including furniture, for free. I believe second-hand furniture would look original and distinctive, and would be more beneficial for the environment, aspects that students would no doubt welcome. The only expense involved would be delivery.

Decor
Many users commented that the decor of the building appeared dated. Materials to improve the decor are relatively affordable, but the cost of labor would put the project over budget. My suggestion is to use student volunteer labor, for both design and physical work. Students from the Design Faculty could be invited to submit designs for different areas of the building, while other students might be asked to volunteer their time to remove the old decor and put up the new.

Conclusion
It should be possible to make improvements to the student union building without going over budget. By thinking creatively and by accessing resources such as freecycling websites, we can make the building more attractive to the majority of users.

B **Look back at the proposal and check the points covered. The writer ...**

1 states a reason for the proposal. ☐
2 uses clear headings to guide the reader. ☐
3 uses quite a formal tone and persuasive language. ☐
4 outlines the consequence of not following the proposal. ☐

C **Read the instructions in the box. Then answer the questions and make notes for a proposal.**

> Your college is planning to improve the student library. A small amount of money is available for the improvements, and you have agreed to write a proposal for the building manager suggesting how the improvements could be made on a small budget.

1 What two aspects of the building could be improved for little expense? Consider these aspects, or use your own ideas.
Outside areas ☐ Decor ☐ Seating ☐ Lighting ☐ Refreshment facilities ☐

____

____

2 For each aspect you have chosen, how specifically could improvements be made for little expense? Make notes of your ideas.

D **Use your notes to from Exercise C to write a proposal. Follow the style of the proposal in Exercise A. Write about 250 words.**

HOW ARE YOU DOING?

◯ I have shown clearly what my proposal is about and who it is for.
◯ I have used polite, persuasive language.
◯ I have used a clear structure, with appropriate headings.

UNIT 2 WATCH THIS SPACE ...

IN THIS UNIT YOU

- learn language to talk about innovation inspired by space exploration
- listen to people from different countries debating the value of space exploration
- write an outline for an essay about life on other planets
- read about how a sci-fi series influenced a modern invention
- talk about the possibility of life on other planets
- learn about evaluating explanations
- watch a video about the search for life on other planets

WRITING
outlining

When you have to write a paragraph or an essay, do you organize what you are going to say? Do you organize your ideas mentally or do you make a written plan?

LISTENING
understanding native English speakers

Do you find it difficult to understand native English speakers from certain countries or regions? If so, which ones?

LIFE SKILLS

STUDY & LEARNING

evaluating explanations Do you usually accept or question explanations that you read or hear ...

- in a book?
- from a friend?
- from a parent or older relative?
- on a website such as Wikipedia?
- in a magazine or newspaper?
- from a teacher or professor?

A How well do you know the universe? Guess the answers to the questions. Then check the answers at the bottom of page 30. Compare your answers with a partner. Whose answers were the closest?

1. The age of the Earth: ______________ years
2. The age of the universe: ______________ years
3. The distance from the Earth to our moon: ______________ kilometers
4. The distance from the Earth to our sun: ______________ kilometers
5. The year that man first landed on the moon: ______________
6. The number of stars visible to the naked eye: ______________
7. The speed of the Earth's rotation at the Equator: ______________ kilometers per hour
8. The year the first mammal (a monkey) went into space: ______________

B Decide which of the statements you agree with and explain why.

Facts like the ones in Exercise A are irrelevant to everyday life. It doesn't matter if people don't have any idea of the answers.

Knowing facts like the ones in Exercise A is important. It gives you a sense of perspective and helps you understand your place in the universe.

1 READING: an online article

A **Read the article. What is the connection between space, science fiction, and cell phones?**

How STAR TREK Inspired an Innovation Your Cell Phone

1 Martin Cooper led the team at Motorola that developed the world's first handheld mobile phone. In the early 1970s, Cooper was worried that Motorola's great rival, AT&T, was gaining a lead in car phone technology and was lobbying the Federal Communications Commission (FCC) for frequency space for its car phone network. Despite the fact that AT&T was larger than Motorola and had much greater research resources, Cooper wanted to challenge and, if possible, to leapfrog the giant. He has said that watching Captain Kirk using his communicator on the television show Star Trek inspired him with a stunning idea—to develop a handheld mobile phone. He and his team took only 90 days in 1973 to create the first portable cellular 800 MHz phone prototype.

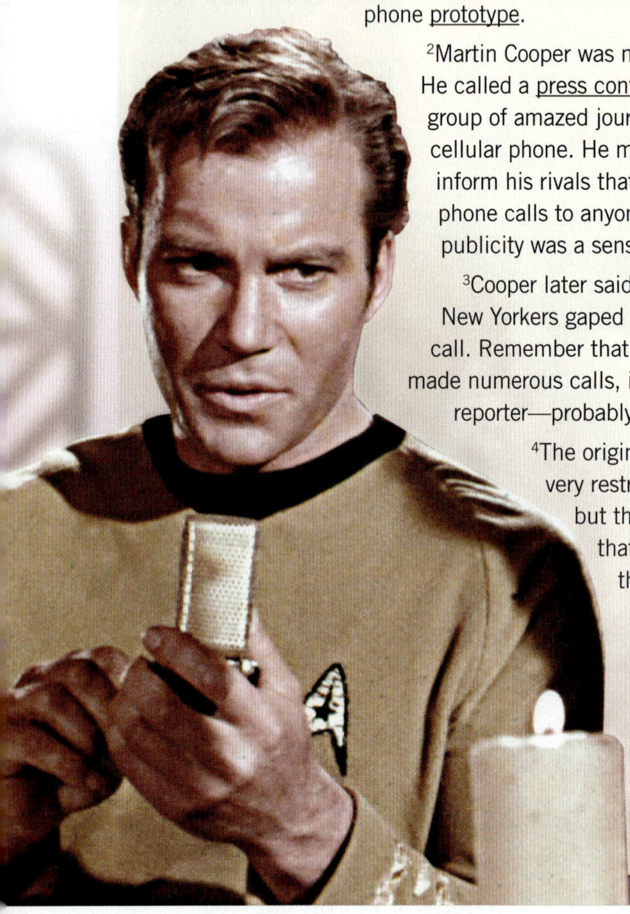

2 Martin Cooper was not just a clever engineer. He also understood the power of public relations. He called a press conference. On April 3, 1973, on Sixth Avenue in New York City, in front of a group of amazed journalists, Cooper made the first public phone call from a prototype handheld cellular phone. He made that first call to Joel Engel, head of research at AT&T Bell Labs, to inform his rivals that they were well behind. He then allowed some of the reporters to make phone calls to anyone of their choosing to prove how the cell phone worked. The resulting publicity was a sensation.

3 Cooper later said, "As I walked down the street while talking on the phone, sophisticated New Yorkers gaped at the sight of someone actually moving around while making a phone call. Remember that in 1973, there weren't cordless telephones, let alone cellular phones. I made numerous calls, including one where I crossed the street while talking to a New York radio reporter—probably one of the more dangerous things I have ever done in my life."

4 The original Motorola DynaTAC handset weighed a hefty 1 kilogram (2.2 lb) and had very restricted talk time. Cooper later joked, "The battery lifetime was 20 minutes, but that wasn't really a big problem because you couldn't hold the phone up for that long." Because of the infrastructure needed, it took a full 10 years before the first commercial cell phone, the DynaTAC 8000x, was launched in 1983. This phone weighed 1.1 pounds (half a kilogram), had 30 minutes of battery life, and was priced at $3,995—about $9,300 in today's prices.

5 The *Star Trek* series foreshadowed many other innovative ideas and inspired other inventors. Ed Roberts, who invented the first home computer, the Altair 8800, named it after the Altair Solar System in a *Star Trek* episode.

www.destination-innovation.com

B **VOCABULARY: BUSINESS AND INNOVATION** **Match the underlined words from the text with their definitions. Change verbs to their base form where necessary.**

1 ______________ (*v.*) to give someone an idea or enthusiasm for doing something
2 ______________ (*n.*) the activity of creating a good opinion of a person, company, or product
3 ______________ (*v.*) to try to influence politicians or people in authority on a particular topic
4 ______________ (*n.*) the first form or example of something new
5 ______________ (*n.*) a very large and successful company
6 ______________ (*v.*) to become more successful or popular than competitors
7 ______________ (*n.*) a set of systems
8 ______________ (*n.*) an official meeting with reporters
9 ______________ (*n.*) a person, team, or business that competes with another
10 ______________ (*v.*) to start selling a new product or service to the public; to send a spacecraft, satellite or other object into space

C **VOCABULARY: BUSINESS AND INNOVATION** Work in small groups. Discuss the questions.

1 Have you heard of AT&T or Motorola? Are these companies giants in the cell phone industry nowadays? Which rival companies are gaining a lead in today's cell phone market?
2 When a company is launching a new product, what kinds of public relations activities do you think are most effective for inspiring young adults to buy it?
3 Can you think of any other inventions that were inspired by science fiction? What kind of new prototypes do you think we might see in the next decade?

2 GRAMMAR: future passive

A **LANGUAGE IN CONTEXT** Read the text. What is the main idea?

a) Science fiction inventions are interesting but not applicable in the real world.
b) Science fiction takes some of its ideas from things in the real world.
c) Some science fiction inventions can be used as ideas for real inventions.

Some really cool things have been created for science fiction movies. Could some of those things actually be invented at some point in the future? Well, did you see the force field, the invisible defense, that protected the starship Enterprise from enemy attacks in *Star Trek*? British military scientists are now working to create force fields to protect their armored vehicles! Short bursts of electrical energy will be activated around the vehicles to make it impossible for bullets to reach them. And what about those robot soldiers in *Avatar*? Apparently, millions of dollars will be spent by the U.S. Department of Defense to develop combat robots. These are just two examples of science fiction items that may be developed for use in the real world in the very near future!

NOTICE!

1 Underline all the examples of the passive in the text.
2 Draw two lines under all the modal verbs.
3 Which of the passive phrases refer to future possibilities? Which are more definite predictions?

B **ANALYZE** Read the text in Exercise A again.

Form **Choose the correct option to complete the rules.**
The future passive is formed with …

a) … *will/may/might/could* + *be* + past participle.
b) … *will/may/might/could* + base form.

C **PRACTICE** Rewrite the active sentences using the future passive. Then look at the pairs of sentences again. Is the active or passive form more suitable? Are both equally suitable? Why? Discuss with a partner.

1 They will invent personal spaceships in the next century.
____

2 We could learn a lot from future science fiction movies.
____

3 Robots will study other planets in my lifetime.
____

4 NASA might train astronauts at a lunar base.
____

5 Do you think people will ever colonize other planets?
____

WATCH OUT!

✘ Force fields will use by the British military.
✓ Force fields will be used by the British military.

D **NOW YOU DO IT** Work in groups. Make a list of things related to space that you think will be done in the next 50 years. Then share your ideas with the class.

We think the moon will be colonized because there are valuable minerals there.

3 LISTENING: understanding native English speakers

English speakers from different countries or regions might speak with different accents. Pay attention to an unfamiliar accent when you hear one and find out where it comes from. The more familiar you are with a range of accents, the better prepared you are to communicate with many different people.

A 1.06 Listen to the people about to attend a book launch. Match the accents that sound the same.

Speaker 1 Speaker 4
Speaker 2 Speaker 5
Speaker 3 Speaker 6

B Listen again and match the speakers with the countries they are from.

India

1 Speakers ___ and ___

U.S.A.

2 Speakers ___ and ___

Australia

3 Speakers ___ and ___

C 1.07 Now listen to the Q & A session after the book launch. Check whether each speaker is *for* or *against* space exploration. Write the main reason for each person's opinion.

Speaker	For	Against	Main reason
1	☐	☐	___
2	☐	☐	___
3	☐	☐	___
4	☐	☐	___
5	☐	☐	___
6	☐	☐	___

D **VOCABULARY: NEGATIVE PREFIXES: *UN-, IN-, IM-*** Complete the table with the correct forms of the words from the box. Then work in pairs and add any other examples you know.

acceptable accurate available aware believable capable certain
measurable patient perfect practical probable significant sufficient

Negative adjectives with *im-*	Negative adjectives with *in-*	Negative adjectives with *un-*
impossible	*insufficient*	*unknown*

E **VOCABULARY: NEGATIVE PREFIXES: *UN-, IN-, IM-*** Work in groups. Discuss whether you think we should continue to explore space. Use reasons from the audio or your own ideas. Include as many words from Exercise D as you can.

4 GRAMMAR: conditional conjunctions

A LANGUAGE IN CONTEXT Read the blog entry. What is the person's general opinion of the possibility of finding life on other planets?

Science Web

Adrian99, Denver, Colorado, U.S.A. → *reply*

I think we have to be very careful in our search for intelligent life on other planets **(1) in case** it's not what we expect. It'll all be fine **(2) as long as** any aliens we contact are peace-loving. **(3) Since** we are uncertain of who or what is out there, I don't think we should be too welcoming. We might be putting the human race in danger **(4) unless** we protect ourselves. However, I do recognize that it could be an amazing cultural experience **(5) provided that** we're careful. Invasion from space might be improbable, but we should make sure we're prepared, **(6) just in case** it actually happens!

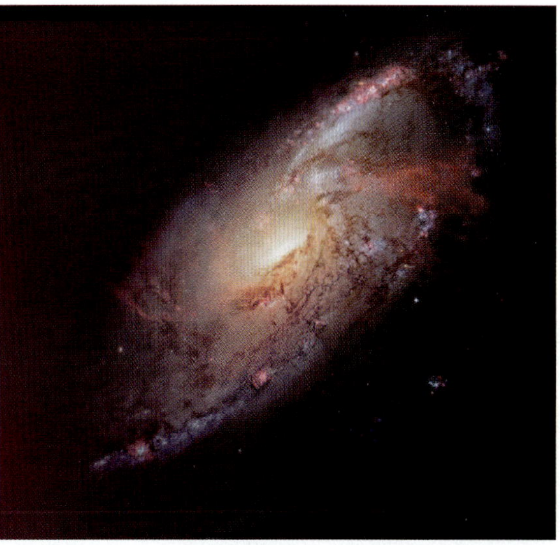

B ANALYZE Read the blog entry in Exercise A again.

Function **Match the numbers of the words and phrases in bold (1–6) with the correct meanings (a–d). Two of the meanings are used twice.**

a) except if ☐
b) only if ☐☐
c) because it is true that ☐
d) because it is possible that ☐☐

Form **Choose the correct option to complete the rule.**
Conditional conjunctions are followed by …
a) a clause (subject + verb). b) a noun.

NOTICE!

Read the three sentences. Which one has a different meaning?

a) We might be putting the human race in danger unless we protect ourselves.
b) We might be putting the human race in danger if we protect ourselves.
c) We might be putting the human race in danger if we don't protect ourselves.

WATCH OUT!

✗ Aliens won't attack us unless we don't attack them.
✓ Aliens won't attack us if we don't attack them.
✓ Aliens won't attack us unless we attack them.

C PRACTICE **Complete each sentence with one word or phrase from Exercise B. In some cases, more than one answer is possible.**

1 We'll never find life on other planets ________ we look for it.
2 We need to be careful about alien encounters ________ they're aggressive.
3 We could learn a lot from an alien culture, ________ we could understand each other.
4 We need to be ready ________ an asteroid or comet is heading toward the Earth.
5 Any message from the stars would take years to reach us ________ they're so far away.
6 The space program will continue ________ there is enough money for it.

D NOW YOU DO IT Work in groups. What do you think will/should happen with space programs in the future? Discuss your ideas with your group.

Provided that …, we will probably …
Unless we …, we might …
As long as …, we should be able to …
We should … in case …
Since …, I think we should …

5 PRONUNCIATION: contrastive stress

A 1.08 Listen to the inference that the stressed words (underlined) add to each sentence.

1 I <u>think</u> there may be life on other planets in our galaxy. = *But I'm uncertain.*
2 I think there may be life on other planets in <u>our</u> galaxy. = *But probably not in other galaxies.*
3 I think there <u>may</u> be life on other planets in our galaxy. = *It's not certain, but it's a real possibility.*
4 <u>I</u> think there may be life on other planets in our galaxy. = *But you may not think so.*
5 I think there may be life on other <u>planets</u> in our galaxy. = *But not on stars or other bodies in the galaxy.*

B Work in pairs. Take turns reading sentences from Exercise A. Listen for the stressed word when your partner reads a sentence. Say which sentence it is (Number 4, etc.).

6 SPEAKING: talking about the possibility of life on other planets

A Read the blog entry. Make notes of the three main reasons why the writer thinks there is no life on other planets.

My Blog: **thought for the day**

IS ANYONE OUT THERE? Print Like it! {10} Comment {3}

[1]A lot of people say that since the universe is such a huge, immeasurable space, it's impossible that we are the only intelligent life forms. Personally, I don't agree. With our sophisticated 21st century communications and radar systems, if there were other intelligent life out there, we would have found it by now. Think of all the technology both here on Earth and on the International Space Station. If that technology hasn't detected other life forms, it's because they're not there.

[2]Some people argue that there is definitely life out there because many people have seen UFOs (Unidentified Flying Objects). However, there has never been any proof of this. Why are there no convincing photos? Obviously, it's because the stories are not true! People like to think that we are not alone in the universe, and they use their imaginations to create all kinds of unbelievable stories. I just don't buy it.

[3]Of course, somewhere in the universe there may be a planet similar to Earth, but so far, all the planets we have found are incapable of supporting any kind of life form. They are either huge balls of gas, like Jupiter and Saturn, or they are too hot or too cold for life to exist on them. Or there is too much or too little gravity. There are many, many factors that had to be exactly right in order for life to evolve on Earth. Maybe another planet like Earth will be formed at some point far in the future, but there are no indications that a planet like this one exists in the present.

B 1.09 Listen to an extract from an interview. Make notes of the three main reasons why the speaker thinks there is probably life on other planets.

C Decide which of the two people in Exercises A and B you agree with more. Add any other arguments you can think of to support that person's view.

D Independent Speaking Work in pairs. Take turns explaining whether you think life on other planets exists or does not exist. Make notes of the main points your partner makes. Report back to the whole class on what your partner said.

7 WRITING: outlining

An outline is a plan of what you are going to write. Making notes of your ideas ensures that the piece of writing is organized properly and you don't forget anything important. Outlines often describe what you plan to put in each paragraph and include topics and supporting details.

A Work in pairs. Read the essay question and the outlines written by two students. Discuss which outline you think is better and say why.

Do you think countries should have space programs? Why or why not?

Paragraph 1: Introduction
- countries that have space programs
- general statement that there are arguments for and against space programs

Paragraph 2: Arguments against space programs
- how money should be spent on Earth
- space program inventions that would have been invented anyway
- need for infrastructure in developing countries, not space programs

Paragraph 3: Arguments for space programs
- inventions that might still be unavailable without space programs
- science and technology advances in developing countries with space programs
- resources on other planets
- job creation due to space programs

Paragraph 4: Conclusion
- arguments for space programs stronger than arguments against them
- summary of main advantages of space programs

Paragraph 1: Introduction
- history of the space program
- my opinion of the space program in my country

Paragraph 2: Arguments against space programs
- amount of money spent on U.S. space program every year
- not all space program inventions useful on Earth
- space programs bad for developing countries

Paragraph 3: Arguments for space programs
- only a few people employed by space programs
- valuable resources on other planets
- more space programs are needed

Paragraph 4: Conclusion
- my opinion—in favor of space programs

Ask yourself ...

- ☐ Do the points in the introduction relate to the general topic?
- ☐ Do all of the points in each section support the topic of the section?
- ☐ Are all of the points specific enough?
- ☐ Does the conclusion summarize the main ideas of the essay?

B Work in pairs. Create an outline for the essay question.

Do you think it is probable or improbable that life exists on other planets?

C Work with another pair. Compare your outlines. Give each other suggestions for improving them.

lifeSkills

EVALUATING EXPLANATIONS

- Understand the difference between correlation and causation.
- Read facts presented by the media and advertisers carefully to see if they are implying that one thing causes another.
- Evaluate explanations of the facts to decide whether claims of causation are accurate or inaccurate.

A Read the extract from an article. In your own words, explain the difference between correlation and causation.

53 | Psychology for You Issue 20.2

ICE CREAM CAUSES SHARK ATTACKS!

by Nathan Kane

We are surrounded by claims. Almost every day in the news you hear stories and statistics that seem to show that A causes B. There are countless examples of headlines claiming that this food causes cancer, or that food prevents it. Understanding and analyzing these claims is an important part of modern life, but we rarely teach it in schools.

We need to teach people to distinguish between correlation and causation. Things "correlate" when they happen together, but it doesn't mean that one causes the other. Let me give you an example. As ice cream sales go up, shark attacks on swimmers go up. This is a fact. So, does this fact mean that ice cream causes people to be eaten by sharks? Of course not! The real explanation is that ice cream sales go up during the summer when the weather is hotter. And people go to the beach more during warm weather, so there are more people in the water for sharks to attack. There's a correlation between the two facts, but that doesn't imply causation. They both happen at the same time, but you have to think a bit more deeply to discover the real cause behind both facts.

B Read each fact and the explanation given. With your class, discuss whether you find the explanation convincing and suggest other possible explanations.

People who play basketball are often taller than average.
Explanation: This is because you need to stretch a lot when playing the game and so you become taller.

Children with bigger hands usually write better.
Explanation: This is because having bigger feet and hands means you can move a pen more easily.

Violent criminals often watch violent movies.
Explanation: This is because watching these movies produces violent feelings and leads people toward crime.

HOW TO SAY IT

I think this explanation is improbable because …

This may be true, provided that …

That can't be right, since …

I think a more likely explanation is that …

C Read the extract from a webpage. Think about whether you tend to agree or disagree with the writer, and say why.

AMERICAN TIMES

Where is everybody?

1 With the news this week that yet more planets have been discovered beyond our solar system, is it just a matter of time before we find someone to say "hello" to? No, says Kelvin Stewart.

2 Although humans have always looked up at the night sky and wondered about what or who might inhabit the tiny, bright worlds they see, it was only in 1960 that modern SETI (the Search for Extraterrestrial Intelligence) began. In that year, the astronomer Frank Drake pointed a radio telescope at two stars, looking for signs of intelligent life, and found ... nothing. Still, that didn't stop him from coming up with his famous "Drake equation." I won't bore you with the math, but the Drake equation basically says, "There are so many billions of stars out there that even if only a tiny fraction of them develop intelligent life, then there must be lots of other intelligent species in our galaxy." But if that's the case, then we should see evidence, or, as physicist Enrico Fermi asked, "Where is everybody?"

3 This is the first key fact about SETI: we haven't heard anything. This is because there's nothing to hear. There are no signals being beamed down to us saying, "Hello, can we be your friends?" because there's no one out there. It's the obvious explanation.

4 The second key fact is that among all the planets we've identified so far, we haven't yet found one capable of sustaining life, like the Earth, outside our solar system. This is because they don't exist. The Earth seems to be unique. It's just the right size and just the right distance from our sun, creating the ideal conditions for life to develop.

5 So, what is it about the search for intelligent life that stops people from seeing this basic logic?

D Work in pairs. The article states two key facts, together with explanations. For each one, discuss how convincing you find the explanation. Make a note of possible alternative explanations.

E Share your ideas with the class. Who has the most convincing explanations for the facts in the text?

F Discuss the questions.

1. What have you learned about evaluating explanations?
2. When you read or hear an explanation for something, what makes you tend to believe it or disbelieve it?

REFLECT ... How can being able to evaluate explanations be useful to you in **Work & Career** and **Self & Society**?

RESEARCH ...

Look for an article about a claim that one thing is caused by another. You could look in these areas:

- health (e.g., "X causes heart disease")
- crime (e.g., "Rise in theft caused by X")
- education (e.g., "X leads to better exam results")
- lifestyle (e.g., "Watching a lot of TV causes X")

When you have found an article, research the topic further and decide if you think there is really causation or simply correlation. Be prepared to tell your class what you found out.

Language wrap-up

1 VOCABULARY

Complete the text with the words and phrases from the box. Make the adjectives negative by using the prefix *un-*, *in-*, or *im-*. (10 points)

available	certain	gained a lead	inspired	known
launched	possible	practical	probable	sufficient

Humans have always wanted to explore **(1)** ________ places, so it is not surprising that we are fascinated by space travel. Writers like Jules Verne were **(2)** ________ to write science fiction stories about space even though space exploration was still **(3)** ________ when they were alive because the technology for it was **(4)** ________ at that time. The "space race" between the U.S.A. and the U.S.S.R. began in the 1950s, and the Soviets **(5)** ________ when they **(6)** ________ a satellite called Sputnik in 1959. The two countries were great rivals for many years. Unfortunately, there is **(7)** ________ money to continue all of the programs related to space exploration, so some of the programs that were considered too **(8)** ________ have been canceled. The future of space travel is **(9)** ________, but there is still hope that one day humans will visit other star systems, even if that seems **(10)** ________ now.

8–10 correct: I can use words for business and innovation and negative prefixes.
0–7 correct: Look again at Sections 1 and 3 on pages 22, 23, and 24. **SCORE:** /10

2 GRAMMAR

Choose the correct option to complete each sentence. (12 points)

1. Astronauts receive training *in case* / *provided that* they have to deal with emergencies.
2. I don't believe life *will be* / *has been* discovered on other planets in the near future.
3. Spacecraft in the future will *design* / *be designed* to travel very long distances.
4. Space tourists might *charge* / *be charged* a lot of money to stay in a hotel on the moon!
5. We won't discover what's out there *unless* / *if* we don't continue to explore.
6. Sending a crew to Mars is possible *as long as* / *in case* we can keep them safe.
7. Do you think a war will ever *fight* / *be fought* in space?
8. NASA may *send* / *be sent* a spacecraft to explore Pluto.
9. I wonder if a colony will *establish* / *be established* on Mars in the future.
10. I'm optimistic about finding extraterrestrial life, *provided that* / *unless* we continue to invest in exploration.
11. I don't think humans could *survive* / *be survived* on any other planet.
12. New forms of space travel may *invent* / *be invented* in the next few years.

10–12 correct: I can use the future passive and conditional conjunctions.
0–9 correct: Look again at Sections 2 and 4 on pages 23 and 25. **SCORE:** /12

Answers to quiz, page 21:

1	4.5 billion years	2	14 billion years	3	384,000 kilometers	4	150 million kilometers
5	1969	6	6,000	7	1,670 kilometers per hour	8	1948

SPEAKING WORKSHOP Describing a picture

A 1.10 **Listen to someone describing a picture of a space colony. Number the main points in the order that they are mentioned from 1–5.**

___ Details about the types of buildings
___ The shape of the colony (round, oval, etc.)
___ The speaker's opinions of life in a space colony
___ Information printed on the picture
___ Details about transportation

B Listen again. Then complete the sentences with the phrases from the box.

appears to be   as long as   look like   says that   shape of   similar to   type of

1 The information at the top of the picture ________ the colony will float in space.
2 The ________ the colony is oval, like a giant egg.
3 There are several structures that ________ airports.
4 These things in the air are ________ cars, but they fly.
5 Many people are … riding a ________ flying bicycle!
6 This strange oval structure ________ some kind of stadium.
7 Living in a space colony will be OK ________ it can be designed to …

C Look at the picture of a different concept for a space colony. Make an outline to prepare a short talk describing the colony. Follow the format in the box.

Intro: Printed info about the picture
- when colony will be built
- where it will be built

General description of the colony
- The dome: shape of dome, how land under dome looks different from land outside of dome
- Description of life in colony: buildings, transportation, what people are doing

Closing: your opinion of what life in a space colony will be like

HOW ARE YOU DOING?

- ◯ I used a logical order to describe the picture.
- ◯ I described a wide range of detail—shapes, activities, positions, etc.
- ◯ I used a variety of vocabulary.

D **Work in pairs. Use your outline to talk about the picture.**

UNIT 3 PASSWORD PROTECTED

IN THIS UNIT YOU

- learn language to talk about issues related to digital security
- read about electronic data collection
- talk about different attitudes toward privacy
- listen to a radio interview about identity theft
- write an email expressing views on a new proposal
- learn about protecting digital privacy
- watch a video about keeping your personal information secure online

READING

text organization

What is the purpose of a persuasive text? Where might you see such a text?

SPEAKING

participating in a group discussion

Why might it be important to keep a group discussion going? What techniques or expressions can you use to keep a discussion going?

LIFE SKILLS

SELF & SOCIETY

protecting digital privacy How many forms of communication (e.g., email) do you use regularly? Are you concerned about digital privacy, and do you take any steps to protect your data? Why or why not?

A Work in pairs. Take the survey. Rate each statement from 1 (doesn't describe you at all) to 5 (describes you very accurately). Share your answers with your partner and give more detail on your responses.

PRIVACY SURVEY

1. I worry that too many people and organizations have private information about me. 1 2 3 4 5
2. I don't talk about what I'm doing on social media. 1 2 3 4 5
3. I never let anyone else use my electronic devices. 1 2 3 4 5
4. I use a different password for every website account. 1 2 3 4 5
5. I almost never use a debit or credit card. 1 2 3 4 5
6. I'm very careful about the information I provide to websites. 1 2 3 4 5
7. I prefer not to buy things online because I don't like giving out my information. 1 2 3 4 5

B Work with another pair. Discuss the questions.

1. Why do you think the issue of privacy receives a lot of attention in the media?
2. If someone looked at all the information about you that exists in cyberspace, what kind of things would they know about you?
3. Do you think this information would give them an accurate impression of your life?

1 READING: text organization page 10

Recognizing the structure of a text you are reading helps you understand the text more quickly. Persuasive texts (texts that try to convince the reader of an opinion) often follow a cause-effect structure. The writer presents causes and explains the effects in order to convince the reader of his or her opinion.

A **Discuss the questions as a class.**

1 What do you think "cyber threat" means?
2 How many different types of cyber threat can you think of?

B **Read the article and discuss the questions in groups.**

1 What does the writer want to persuade the reader to think?
2 What information does the writer use to persuade the reader?
3 Do you think the article will convince readers to agree with the writer? Why or why not?

OUR DATA IS NOT OUR OWN!

by Stephen Shaw

1 Every time you make a call on your cell phone, data is collected about where you are, who you're calling, and even what direction you're traveling in. Credit card payments leave detailed records of your purchases. We're told that monitoring online activity prevents crime, helps in the fight against terrorism, and makes life easier for all of us. However, high-profile news stories about the amount of data that is collected on all of us, as well as numerous incidents of hacking into retailers' databases, have highlighted the risk we're taking by allowing others to invade our privacy like this.

2 We should all be concerned about online security to prevent criminals from getting our personal information because data theft can create horrifying problems. There have been a number of high-profile cases where employees have lost mobile devices containing the data of thousands of customers, or where criminals have hacked into databases. The most common consequence of this sort of thing is identity theft, when criminals get credit card or bank account numbers and spend a lot of money in another person's name. Another problem is internet scams where criminals send you an email saying that you've won a lot of money, and you just need to send them your bank details so that they can put the money in your account. Finally, some people are left open to blackmail when information about their private lives falls into the wrong hands.

3 Even if the information doesn't fall into the hands of criminals, there is still the possibility that it will be shared among different companies or different authorities. What are the possible effects of that? It means that information collected for one purpose could be used for a completely different purpose. We might be happy with an airline collecting information about us in the belief that this helps to prevent terrorism. However, what if that information is then shared with other companies, who use it to direct their ads at us more efficiently? Are you happy with your personal data being used in that way?

4 Then there's the question of what happens if we do nothing about the situation. There are valid reasons why companies and governments need to compile certain information about people's lives, but the result of this is that they keep demanding more and more information. Unless we all exert more control over our personal data, we will soon find that there is no aspect of our private lives that is not in some way recorded, stored, used, and potentially abused.

5 From store loyalty cards to electronic travel cards, and from emails to text messages, our everyday lives create an enormous amount of information, and it's difficult to see how we can change that. We live, after all, in the information age. However, we can affect what happens to the information we produce. By demanding to know why our data is being collected and how it's being used, we can all take back some of the control over our private lives.

C The table represents the functions of the five paragraphs in the article. Read the article again and complete the table.

	Function	
1	Introduction: The size and scope of the problem is explained, with specific examples.	
2	Cause: data theft	Effects: identity theft, ________, ________
3	Cause: information sharing	Effect: ________
4	Cause: ________ ________	Effect: ________, ________
5	Conclusion: Summary of the situation and call to action	

D VOCABULARY: DIGITAL PRIVACY Complete the sentences with the words and phrases from the box.

blackmail compile database hack identity theft information age invade your privacy leave (someone) open to monitor scam

1 I believe nobody should have the right to ________ without your permission.
2 I don't worry about the fact that corporations ________ information on each of us all the time.
3 If you don't protect your digital privacy, you may ________ yourself ________ theft by cyber criminals.
4 In the ________ that we now live in, data is worth money.
5 Internet search engines ________ what customers are looking at online to get information they can sell to advertisers.
6 ________ is the most common cyber crime these days, so we should be careful about putting our documents online.
7 Cyber criminals know how to ________ into databases and steal secret information.
8 Criminals are sometimes able to ________ people for a lot of money by threatening to do something to them or their families.
9 My brother lost a lot of money in an internet ________!
10 Companies often keep a ________ with all their customers' details in it.

E VOCABULARY: DIGITAL PRIVACY Work in pairs. Decide whether you agree or disagree with the statements. Explain why.

1 A certain amount of surveillance and invasion of our privacy makes us safer.
2 You should never shop online because you leave yourself open to crimes like identity theft.
3 Companies should be allowed to monitor online activity and sell their databases.

2 WRITING: a persuasive email

A 1.11 Read the notice on a college website. Then listen to the conversation. What points do the students make in favor of and against the proposal?

NOTICE TO STUDENTS WITH CREDIT CARDS

There is a proposal for a new state law that would allow parents to monitor their kids' online credit card purchases as long as their children are in college and under 21. We want to know your opinion, so please write to us at: theuopinions@theu.edu.

B Write an email to the website explaining what you think the effects of the proposed law will be. Try to persuade readers to agree with you.

3 GRAMMAR: object complements

A LANGUAGE IN CONTEXT Read the text. What advice does the writer give? Do you usually follow this advice?

NOTICE!

Circle the direct objects in the text. Does a direct object come after a noun or a verb?

Protect Your Identity

Identity thieves are out there, and they're after your data! Too many of us consider our personal information secure, and we don't see identity theft as a problem. However, if you don't keep your data secret, a criminal can find it very easy to steal money from you. This can make your life very hard, and it can be extremely difficult to prove yourself an innocent victim. Never throw personal documents in the garbage. Always shred anything that contains private information.

B ANALYZE Read the text in Exercise A again.

Form **Read the explanation and examples. Then find and underline six object complements in the text in Exercise A.**

After some verbs, we can provide information about the object of a sentence using an object complement. The object complement may be an adjective or a noun. Some verbs take only an adjective, some take only a noun, and some can take either one. After verbs that say how we see or describe something or someone, we often use *as*.

Form	Examples
subject + verb + object + adjective	*We don't consider him **dangerous**.* *I found the situation **unacceptable**.* *You should keep it **private**.*
subject + verb + object + noun	*They should make this **a priority**.* *The writer called him **a criminal**.* *They finally proved him **a thief**.*
subject + verb + object + *as* + noun / adjective	*She described him **as trustworthy**.* *We know him **as an honest man**.* *I don't see it **as a problem**.*

WATCH OUT!

✗ You can't call you an expert on this topic.
✓ You can't call yourself an expert on this topic.

C PRACTICE Rewrite each sentence using the word in parentheses and a structure from Exercise B.

1 Do you think identity theft is very common? (*consider*)

____

2 You can't just say you are a police officer! (*call*)

____

3 Do you think invasion of privacy is a major problem? (*see*)

____

4 It's not always easy to show that an ID is fake. (*prove*)

____

5 The press says she is a great leader. (*describes*)

____

6 Did you think the article was interesting? (*find*)

____

D NOW YOU DO IT Work in pairs. Think about how you would complete the sentences. Then compare your ideas with your partner.

1 It makes me … when …
2 I find the whole question of electronic data collection …
3 I consider identity theft a/an … issue because …
4 Governments should make … a priority.

4 LISTENING: to an interview

A Read the extract from an entertainment guide. What do you think happened to Justine when her identity was stolen?

Radio Guide **Thursday 6:00 p.m.** ***The Whole Story***

This week's *The Whole Story* (Public Radio, 88.6 FM) looks at the growing problem of identity theft. It features an interview with Justine Black, whose identity was stolen after thieves hacked into an online database of customers of a well-known store. Her story raises the question of whether any of us are actually safe online.

B 1.12 Listen to the interview. As you listen, choose T (true) or F (false).

1 Justine has gotten herself into a lot of debt. T / F
2 She found out about the identity theft immediately. T / F
3 She found it difficult to convince the bank of her innocence. T / F
4 Her own carelessness probably caused the problem. T / F
5 Justine may still face further identity problems in the future. T / F

C **VOCABULARY: PHRASAL VERBS** Listen to the interview again. Complete the phrasal verbs with the prepositions from the box. Some of the prepositions can be used more than once.

of on out through up

1 call ____________
2 take ____________
3 run ____________
4 end ____________
5 get hold ____________
6 get out ____________
7 clear ____________
8 go ____________

D **VOCABULARY: PHRASAL VERBS** Complete the sentences with the correct form of the phrasal verbs from Exercise C. In pairs, discuss what each phrasal verb means and give one more example of how to use each one.

1 I want to ____________ some good anti-piracy software, but I don't know how.
2 The thief used my cell phone abroad and ____________ a huge bill.
3 After losing thousands of dollars in an internet scam, Edward had to ____________ a loan to pay his rent before the matter was ____________ and he got his money back.
4 A group of identity theft victims is ____________ the government to do more to prevent cyber crime.
5 Some people will do anything to ____________ paying their bills.
6 I'm very cautious about putting information online now; I've been a victim of identity theft once and I don't want to ____________ that again.
7 If you start worrying too much about internet security, you'll ____________ being too scared to do anything online.

5 PRONUNCIATION: connected speech—final consonant sound to first vowel sound

A 1.13 Listen to the phrasal verbs. Notice how the final consonant sound of the first word sounds like it is connected to the first vowel sound of the second word. Listen again and practice saying the phrasal verbs.

Phrase:	end up	get out	take out	run up	call on	clear up	look at
Sounds like:	/en-'dʌp/	/ge-'daʊt/	/teɪ-'kaʊt/	/rʌ-'nʌp/	/'kɔ-lɑn/	/klɪ-'rʌp/	/'lʊ-kæt/

B 1.14 Listen to the sentences. Practice saying them using connected speech. Then practice the sentences with a partner.

1 If you take out lots of credit cards, you might run up a lot of debt.
2 If you end up in debt, it's hard to get out of it.
3 Sometimes you have to call on an expert to clear up questions.

6 GRAMMAR: negative structures with *think*, *suppose*, etc.

A 1.15 **LANGUAGE IN CONTEXT** **Listen to the conversation. How does Maca's attitude to privacy differ from Susan's?**

Susan: Are you going to post these photos on Facebook?
Maca: I don't think so. I don't use Facebook anymore. I don't feel that everyone needs to know what I'm doing all the time.
Susan: Seriously? I didn't think there was anyone who wasn't on Facebook! You're probably the only one.
Maca: I'm not so sure. I don't expect I'm the only person who doesn't want to have a huge digital footprint.
Susan: Well, I guess not, but I don't suppose many people actually think about their digital footprint.
Maca: Yeah, I don't imagine so, but people really shouldn't give out so much personal information. It leaves them open to problems.
Susan: True. I guess I shouldn't post about everything I do.

B ANALYZE **Read the conversation in Exercise A again.**

NOTICE!
Circle six different opinion verbs in the conversation. Which of the verbs have other meanings apart from feelings or opinions?

Form & Function **Choose the correct options to complete the rules. Then complete the table with examples from the conversation.**

When we express negative opinions with words like *think* or *believe*, we usually make the *first* / *second* verb negative. With verbs like *hope*, *guess*, *suspect*, and *assume*, we usually make the *first* / *second* verb negative. With verbs like *suppose* or *expect*, we can make the *first* / *second* / *either* verb negative.

Verbs	Affirmative	Negative
think, believe, imagine, feel	*I feel that everyone needs to know …* *I thought everyone was on Facebook!*	(1) ____ (2) ____
hope, guess, suspect, assume	*I guess I should post about everything …*	(3) ____
suppose, expect	*I suppose many people think about …* *I expect I'm the only person …*	(4) ____ (5) ____

Negative short answers

Verbs	Affirmative	Negative
think, believe, imagine	*I imagine so.*	(6) ____
hope, guess, suspect, assume	*I guess so.*	(7) ____
suppose, expect	*I suppose so.*	*I suppose not. / I don't suppose so.*

C PRACTICE **Complete each response with negative forms using the words and phrases in parentheses.**

1 "Are people careful enough on social networking sites such as Facebook?"
"No, I ____________ (*suspect*). I ____________ (*hope / identity theft / increase*)."
2 "Are attitudes toward privacy the same now as in the past?"
"No, I ____________ (*think*). I ____________ (*believe / opinions / stay*) the same forever."
3 "Do you think people will give up all privacy in the future?"
"Well, I ____________ (*hope*). I ____________ (*imagine / people / will give up*) their privacy easily."
4 "Does Twitter play a big part in your life?"
"No, I ____________ (*guess*). I ____________ (*feel / it / help*) me communicate with people."

D **NOW YOU DO IT** **Work in pairs. Ask and answer the questions from Exercise C.**

7 SPEAKING: participating in a group discussion

In a group discussion, it's important to keep the conversation moving. At the same time, everyone in the group should get to express their opinion. We use various phrases for keeping the discussion moving, for politely interrupting a speaker, to focus on relevant points, and to invite contributions.

A 1.17 **Listen to a group discussing how ideas of privacy differ. As you listen, check the points that are mentioned.**

1 I don't want anyone to invade my privacy. ☐
2 I share more information online than my parents. ☐
3 People have less respect for privacy nowadays. ☐
4 Different cultures view privacy differently. ☐
5 Opinions about privacy depend on people's experiences. ☐

B Listen again. Then complete the phrases.

Starting, finishing, and keeping the discussion moving:
Why don't we **(1)** ________________ by talking/thinking about …
Maybe we should **(2)** ________________ to talking/thinking about …
(3) ________________ let's make a note of …
The next point for discussion is …

Interrupting politely:
(4) ________________ to stop you, but maybe we should focus on …
I don't mean to interrupt you, but the issue is …

Inviting contributions:
Does anyone want to **(5)** ________________ anything on the topic of …
I'd be interested to know what you think about …
I don't think we've heard from …

C Work in groups. Discuss points 1–3. Use the phrases from Exercise B to manage the discussion. Report back to the class on your discussion.

1 Your attitude toward privacy in general
2 How you feel about online privacy
3 How you expect privacy to be affected by technology in the future

A: *Why don't we start by talking about our own attitudes toward privacy?*
B: *OK, that sounds good. I can begin. I'm not too concerned about privacy. I love sharing what I'm doing and what I'm thinking. And I like knowing what my friends are doing, too. It makes me feel connected all the time, but I don't imagine that everyone else feels the same way about it.*
C: *Yeah, I don't suppose everyone agrees with you. For example, I don't think …*

lifeSkills

PROTECTING DIGITAL PRIVACY

- Understand the potential threats to digital privacy.
- Think about practical steps to take to increase digital security.
- Take measures to keep your online data secure.

A **Think about the online services and accounts you use (email, Twitter, Facebook, Amazon, etc.). Check which of these pieces of information about you it might be possible to find online.**

your full name	☐	your email address	☐	your birth date	☐
your ID number	☐	your address	☐	the place where you work/study	☐
your phone number	☐	your credit card number	☐	family member names	☐
bank account number	☐				

Protect Yourself *Online*

B **Work in pairs. Look at your answers to Exercise A. Discuss the possible consequences of this online information getting into the wrong hands. Make a list.**

People could send spam to my email address.

C **Work in pairs. Read the article. Student A, explain in your own words what advice is given regarding software and browsers. Student B, explain in your own words what advice is given about email, secure payments, and privacy policies.**

Your personal information is valuable—and you should make it a priority to protect your privacy. Here are some online safety tips to help you protect your personal information and secure your computer.

YOUR SOFTWARE Use anti-virus, anti-spyware, and firewall software—and make sure it's up-to-date. Anti-virus software protects your computer from viruses that can allow people to hack into your computer. Spyware is a software program installed on your computer without your consent to monitor your behavior online or record your keystrokes. Anti-spyware software can remove or disable spyware. Firewalls help keep hackers from getting access to your computer to send out your personal information without your permission.

YOUR BROWSER Configure your browser or operating system to manage pop-ups, cookies, or block specific websites.

YOUR EMAIL Use a separate email address for online transactions. Keep the inbox you use to communicate with friends and family free of spam by using a separate email address when you fill in forms as you shop or conduct other transactions online.

SECURE PAYMENTS When paying for anything online, make sure the transaction is secure. Look for the padlock symbol in the status bar at the bottom of your browser. This will keep criminals from getting hold of your card details and running up debts in your name.

PRIVACY POLICIES When visiting a website for the first time, always make sure the site has a posted privacy policy—and read it. It should explain how your personal data will be collected and used or shared with other parties. If a website doesn't have a privacy policy, consider doing business elsewhere.

Self and Society
Work and Career
Study and Learning

D Work in groups. Read the question posted on an online forum. Discuss what advice you would give the writer and make a list of key points. Share your ideas with the whole class.

greenhorn92

registered:
October 12

posts: 51

Hi, guys,

I've been reading about protecting my privacy online, and I was hoping you could give me some ideas about how to increase my personal security. The thing I'm most interested in is passwords. Any tips out there on making up secure passwords and things like that? I don't want to end up having the problems some of my friends have had!

Thanks!

Monday, March 27 5:40 p.m.

E Work in groups. Make a list of the top three pieces of advice you would give to someone concerned about online privacy. Then create a combined class list of advice.

F Discuss the questions.

1 What have you learned about protecting digital privacy?
2 Considering what you've discussed, are you planning to make any changes to your online habits? If so, what?

HOW TO SAY IT

To keep your password secure, you should …

I don't think you need to …

We consider a good password one that …

You should make it a priority to …

I've found it helpful to …

REFLECT … How can knowing how to protect your digital privacy be useful to you in **Work & Career** and **Study & Learning**?

RESEARCH …

Find an example of an internet scam or another type of cybercrime and tell your class about it. You can find people's stories on the internet, or you may know someone personally who has been a victim of this type of crime.

Language wrap-up

1 VOCABULARY

Complete the paragraph with the words from the box. (12 points)

clear up compiled databases end up get hold of hack identity theft information age leaves us open privacy run up take out

We live in the **(1)** ________________, and as we conduct more and more of our lives online, the increased danger of other people invading our **(2)** ________________ has become a hot issue. Many people argue that companies have **(3)** ________________ too much data about their customers and that this **(4)** ________________ to cyber crime. They point to the fact that the information is often kept on **(5)** ________________ that are far from secure, and which criminals can easily **(6)** ________________ into to **(7)** ________________ information like our bank account numbers. This may allow them to use our information to **(8)** ________________ credit cards and **(9)** ________________ huge debts in our names. **(10)** ________________ is now one of the most common crimes, and it can take years to **(11)** ________________ the problems that this causes. People can even **(12)** ________________ having to pay debts that they didn't create!

10–12 correct: I can use words and phrasal verbs connected to privacy.
0–9 correct: Look again at Sections 1 and 4 on pages 34, 35, and 37. **SCORE:** /12

2 GRAMMAR

A Choose the correct option to complete each sentence. (5 points)

1 "Did anyone see your password?" "No, I *think not* / *don't think so*."
2 "I *assume he doesn't know* / *don't assume he knows* my password."
3 "Do you change your password often enough?" "No, I *guess not* / *don't guess so*."
4 "I *think not you* / *don't think you are* careful enough about keeping your password secret."
5 "Has anyone hacked into your account?" "I *hope not* / *don't hope so*."

B Put the words in the correct order to form sentences. (5 points)

1 all / we / priority / to make / privacy / need / a / .

____

2 careful / to keep / I'm / private / some things / .

____

3 paranoid / me / can call / you / but / never / use / I / public computers / .

____

4 privacy / as / describe / you / would / important / to you / ?

____

5 finally / guilty / him / they / found / identity theft / of / .

____

8–10 correct: I can use object complements and negative structures, including negative short answers.
0–7 correct: Look again at Sections 3 and 6 on pages 36 and 38. **SCORE:** /10

WRITING WORKSHOP

Writing a for-and-against essay

A Read the essay question about using social media and the answer. Is the writer generally in favor of social media or against it? How do you know?

Do you believe that social media has primarily positive or negative effects on society? Give reasons for your opinion.

1We live in the information age, and these days there are very few people, especially young people, who do not consider social media an important part of their lives. However, the fact that many people use social media does not mean that it is a positive development for society.

2Of course, there are good arguments in favor of social media. People can find old friends that they had lost contact with. It's easy to stay in touch with friends and family who live far away, and you can easily share photos or videos with them, which makes people feel closer to each other.

3However, there are a number of problems with social media. Because people want to be connected 24/7, many people now spend more time communicating with their electronic devices than in person. The effect of this is that communication is becoming very impersonal. Also, when you use social media, you put an enormous amount of information about yourself into cyberspace for anyone to see. That can result in data theft or even blackmail. Finally, people are spending more and more time using electronic devices, and less and less time doing physical activities. This is contributing to a worldwide obesity problem.

4To summarize, although using social media allows us to communicate easily, it has many disadvantages. Therefore, I believe that people should reduce the amount of time they spend using social media. Furthermore, they should be very careful about how much information they share with the world.

B Look at the essay again and find these things.

Paragraph 1:
- The main idea of the whole essay.

Paragraph 2:
- The topic sentence of the paragraph. Is this in favor of or against the main idea?
- Points that support the topic sentence. How many points are there?

Paragraph 3:
- The topic sentence of the paragraph. Is this in favor of or against the main idea?
- Points that support the topic sentence. How many points are there?

Paragraph 4:
- A general statement of the writer's opinion.

C Make notes for a four-paragraph essay to answer the question below, using the bullet points to help you.

Do you think governments and businesses should be allowed to collect data such as what phone numbers we call, what we buy and where we shop, and what types of searches we do on the internet? Why or why not?

- the main idea of the whole essay
- the topic sentence of paragraph 2
- points that support the topic sentence
- the topic sentence of paragraph 3
- points that support the topic sentence
- a general statement of your opinion

D Use your notes to write your essay. Write about 250 words.

HOW ARE YOU DOING?

- ◯ I have stated my general opinion in the introduction and re-stated it in the conclusion.
- ◯ I have written one paragraph for the topic and one paragraph against the topic.
- ◯ I have used words of addition (*furthermore*, *also*) and cause-effect (*because*, *as a result*).

UNIT 4 A NEW LOOK AT LEARNING

IN THIS UNIT YOU

- learn language to talk about educational trends
- listen to people debate the merits of online learning
- write a variety of sentence types to describe a personal experience
- read about the value of a college degree
- talk about changes and new alternatives in education
- learn about anticipating cultural differences
- watch a video about the use of technology in the classroom

WRITING

sentence variety

Why might you want to include different types of sentences in your writing? What are some effects of using either short or long sentences?

LISTENING

understanding non-native English speakers

What are some challenges you might face listening to a conversation between non-native speakers of English?

LIFE SKILLS

SELF & SOCIETY

anticipating cultural differences

Do you ever meet people from different cultures? What kind of differences do you observe?

A Work in pairs. Look at the pictures and read the statements. Decide which of the areas listed in the box each statement relates to. You may decide that some or all of the statements relate to more than one area.

Education	Globalization	"Soft skills" like critical thinking	Technology

1

"We are currently preparing students for jobs that don't yet exist, using technologies not yet invented, in order to solve problems we don't even know are problems yet."
–Karl Fisch

2

There are three times as many non-native speakers of English as there are native speakers.

3

"We can't solve problems by using the same kind of thinking we used when we created them."
–Albert Einstein

B Work in groups. Discuss the questions.

1 Choose one of the statements. What issues can you think of connected to this statement? How do they relate to your life now?
2 What are the general implications of the statements for your future?

1 SPEAKING: talking about educational alternatives

A Work in pairs. Read the article. Discuss whether the author is in favor of or against virtual degree programs.

ITHACAUNIVERSITY INVESTIGATES NEW LEARNING DEVELOPMENTS

THE ONLINE ALTERNATIVE

June 20th | 14 Comments

Not all students are alike. This may seem obvious, but it is something that our school systems, including universities, do not take into account enough. Students are all expected to learn and behave in a similar way, and though this may work for many students, it certainly doesn't work for everyone. The college dropout rate in the U.S.A. (students who do not finish a four-year degree program) is just a little less than 50%. Students drop out of college for a number of reasons, and most dropouts never get a chance to go back and finish their degrees.

In spite of this depressing statistic, there is now increasing hope that more students will get a college degree. Many universities in the U.S.A. are now offering online degree programs, a viable alternative to the traditional on-campus college. Virtual universities are offering a broad range of courses at very affordable prices. This makes virtual degree programs a good alternative for students who can't afford to pay the high tuition fees of traditional universities and don't want to get into debt by taking out huge student loans. They are also a practical solution for students who live too far away from the college where they want to study. Online programs foster skills such as self-discipline, decision-making, and time management. Students choose their own classes, set their own schedule, and report to a professor by phone or online. They can organize their studying however they want. Virtual students are not faced with the social distractions and peer pressure that on-campus students have to deal with, and they receive individualized tutoring from their faculty advisor. In addition, more universities are now offering free online courses that allow the student to get a taste of the topic before signing up for a full degree program. Online universities may be the answer for many people who want to get a college education, but can't or don't want to attend a traditional university.

B VOCABULARY: VERB COLLOCATIONS Find examples in the text in Exercise A to complete the lists of collocations.

1 take into: consideration, ______________
2 get: a chance, a college degree, ______________, ______________, ______________
3 drop out of: a class, a group, ______________
4 offer a broad range of: choices, products, alternatives, classes, ______________
5 set: goals, a date, a time, ______________
6 be faced with: problems, ______________, ______________

C VOCABULARY: VERB COLLOCATIONS Work in groups. Discuss the questions.

1 Do many students drop out of college in your country? Why or why not?
2 What kinds of problems and decisions are college students often faced with?
3 What should you take into consideration when deciding where and what to study?

D 1.17 Listen to the radio broadcast. Take notes on the ways the guest speaker disagrees with the opinion in the article in Exercise A.

E Consider the opinions from Exercises A and D. What do you think of online colleges? Write notes to prepare a short talk.

F Independent Speaking Work in pairs. Take turns to explain your opinions. Were they similar or different?

2 GRAMMAR: relative pronouns with *–ever*

A LANGUAGE IN CONTEXT **Read the discussion thread for a distance education class. Which students don't feel confident? Why?**

Forums > General Discussion > Introductions

Luc Auchêne
Hello from Geneva, Switzerland. I hope I can keep up with this class. I'm very busy—I have a full-time job, and we have a new baby. I guess I'll just study whenever I can. Wish me luck!

Ji-Hyun
Congratulations on the birth of your child, Luc! I know what you mean about being busy, but whatever you do, don't panic! The thing I love about an online course is that I can study whenever I want—and however I want! In my pajamas, with music on, while eating ... It's great.

Abdelrahim Alhamadi
Can someone please help me to register? Whatever password I try to choose is rejected!

NOTICE!
Underline the words in Exercise A that end with ***–ever***, such as ***wherever***? How are these words formed?

B ANALYZE **Read the discussion thread in Exercise A again.**

Function **Choose the correct option to complete the rule.**
Whatever, *whenever*, *however*, *whoever*, and *wherever* are used to talk about
a) a known, specific time, place, thing, or person
b) an unknown, general time, place, thing, or person

Form **Complete the table with examples from the text.**

Pronoun	Followed by	Example
1 whatever	subject + verb object + subject + verb	... **(1)** ________, don't panic! **(2)** ________ is rejected.
2 whoever	verb	Whoever designed this program did a good job.
3 whenever, however, wherever	subject + verb	You can put the books wherever you like on the shelves. I can study **(3)** ________ and **(4)** ________.

C PRACTICE **Put the words in the correct order to form sentences.**

1 take / I go / me wherever / I can / my tablet / with / .
____
2 whatever / you / want / can study / language you / .
____
3 have time / students / they / whenever / can study / .
____
4 to study / you choose / however / it's / up to you / .
____
5 log on, I / an error message / I try to / get / whenever / .
____

WATCH OUT!
✗ Whatever I want to buy are too expensive.
✓ Whatever I want to buy is too expensive.

D NOW YOU DO IT **Work in groups. Discuss the questions.**

1 What would you like about an online class?
2 What would be challenging?

If you take an online course, you can ... whenever/whatever/however you want.

3 PRONUNCIATION: vowel length before final consonant sounds

A 1.18 Listen to the word pairs. Notice that vowel sounds are longer before voiced consonant sounds than before voiceless consonant sounds.

Voiceless:	hurt	late	rope	cup	back	pick	safe	life	close	Miss
Voiced:	heard	laid	robe	cub	bag	pig	save	live	close	Ms.

B 1.19 Listen and practice the sentences. Pay attention to vowel length. Then practice the sentences with a partner.

1 I heard you got hurt in the chemistry lab.
2 The teaching assistant got laid off for being late.
3 The college library is close, but it's about to close.
4 The university orchestra played the best live music I've heard in my life.
5 When I got back to class, my bag was gone.
6 Ms. Taylor hates being called Miss Taylor.

4 LISTENING: understanding non-native English speakers page 24

Non-native speakers of English with different first languages sometimes use different stress, intonation patterns, and sounds, which you may not be familiar with. Identifying things that cause difficulties can help you understand other non-native speakers.

A 1.20 Listen to three conversations and write the main idea of each one. Then work in pairs and discuss whether you found it easy to identify the topic.

1 Main idea: ____________________
2 Main idea: ____________________
3 Main idea: ____________________

B Listen again. Which speaker did you find easier to understand in each conversation? Choose the reason(s) why you think it was easier.

- ☐ The accent sounds the same as or similar to mine.
- ☐ He/She uses sounds that I have in my language.
- ☐ The accent is one that I'm already familiar with.
- ☐ He/She spoke more slowly.
- ☐ Other: ____________________

C Work in groups. Discuss the questions.

1 What makes an accent (either native or non-native English) easier or more difficult for you to understand?
2 What are some strategies you can use when you are having trouble understanding someone's accent?
3 What are some actions you can take if you suspect someone is having trouble understanding your accent?

5 GRAMMAR: mixed conditionals

A 1.21 **LANGUAGE IN CONTEXT** **Listen to the conversation. In what ways is technology changing education, according to the speakers?**

Ruth: Wow. This article says that a large percentage of what you learn in college in any technical field will be obsolete by the time you graduate.

Patrick: Whoa, so if I had studied engineering, my degree might be obsolete by now.

Pete: Technology is changing everything. If my college weren't so high-tech, I wouldn't have been able to do international online projects. That experience helped me get this job.

Katrin: I agree. I studied at a more traditional college, and my computer skills aren't that great. If I had better IT skills, I probably would have gotten a better job. At least I know English. If I hadn't learned English, I don't think I would have *any* job!

NOTICE!

Find the sentences that contain the word ***if***. Underline the ***if*** clause and circle the result clause. Do the sentences follow the usual structure of 2nd or 3rd conditionals?

B **ANALYZE** **Read the conversation in Exercise A again.**

Form & Function **Complete the table with examples from the conversation. Then choose the correct options to complete the table.**

Function	Example	Mixed conditional form
For a current or general situation with a past result	If my college weren't so high-tech, I wouldn't have been able to do international online projects. If I **(1)** ________ better IT skills, I probably **(2)** ________ a better job.	*If* clause in **(3)** *2nd* / *3rd* conditional, result clause in **(4)** *2nd* / *3rd* conditional (*If* + simple past, … *would/could/may/might have* + past participle)
For a past event or situation with a present result	If I had studied engineering, my college degree might be obsolete by now! If I **(5)** ________ English, I don't think I **(6)** ________ any job!	*If* clause in **(7)** *2nd* / *3rd* conditional, result clause in **(8)** *2nd* / *3rd* conditional (*If* + past perfect, … *would/could/may/might* + infinitive)

C **PRACTICE** **Combine the sentence pairs to make mixed conditional sentences.**

1 Your cousin isn't good at taking exams. He didn't pass the college entrance exam.
If my cousin were ________

2 Your sister didn't study hard in college. She doesn't have a good job now.
If my sister had ________

3 The college doesn't offer a degree in management. You didn't apply to study there.
____

4 Your uncle doesn't keep up with changes in technology. He lost his job.
____

5 You didn't stay at your old job. You are not a department manager there now.
____

6 The internet didn't exist 40 years ago. Your dad doesn't use it as well as you do.
____

WATCH OUT!

✗ If I didn't know English, I hadn't gotten into this university.

✓ If I didn't know English, I wouldn't have gotten into this university.

D **NOW YOU DO IT** **Work in pairs. Talk about how technology has affected your education. Think about:**

- something you did recently that you wouldn't have been able to do if the internet didn't exist
- something you would be better at now if you had had the technology for it when you were younger.

6 READING: a statistics-based argument

A Read the article. What is the author's main point? How are statistics used to support that point?

Is it worth it?

[1]In a world where an increasing number of people go through higher education, your college degree no longer makes you stand out in the way it used to. Almost 32% of young adults get a Bachelor's degree or higher in the U.S.A., and the national average cost of that four-year degree is estimated to be over $100,000 for public colleges, rising to many times that for some of the more outstanding private colleges. As a result, there is a legitimate question over whether a college standard of education is really worth it.

[2]In fact, the question really is: Worth it to whom? First, we have state and national governments, who invest heavily in education and look for social returns on that investment. From where they stand, it's important that increased levels of higher education produce tangible benefits, which indeed they often do. College graduates tend to be healthier, smoke less, and do more exercise than their less educated peers, and so they cost less in healthcare. They are more likely to vote, and only 4% of them live in poverty and require government support. In addition, college graduates tend to contribute more in taxes as a result of higher earnings.

[3]Indeed, the primary benefit to graduates themselves is that they stand to reap high financial rewards from a college education. Research shows that the average high school graduate will currently earn around $1.7 million over their working life, while the average college graduate with a Bachelor's degree earns roughly 94% more, at $3.3 million. As well as approximately doubling lifetime earnings, holding a Bachelor's degree halves the chance that you will be unemployed. In fact, it is predicted that by 2020 you will need a college education to even stand a chance of getting 63% of all jobs in the U.S. It stands to reason, then, that for those who can afford the initial costs, getting a college degree makes good financial sense.

[4]However, higher income is not guaranteed for all. Graduates in areas such as engineering, computers, and math can expect to earn up to 50% more than the average for all college graduates, while those in areas such as education may earn significantly less. Education majors who work in service jobs may actually earn around $1.3 million over their lifetimes—less than the average for high school graduates.

[5]Overall then, the question is still open. While the benefit to society seems clear, the value to the individual, at least in monetary terms, will depend on many factors, including where and what you choose to study. Ultimately, answering the question of whether a particular course is worth it is a very personal calculation, based on the importance you attach to income level, social standing, and personal fulfilment.

B VOCABULARY: WORDS RELATED TO *STAND* Match the words and phrases with the correct definitions. Use the contexts from the article in Exercise A to help you.

1 from where someone stands (*phr. para 2*)
2 stand to do (*v. para 3*)
3 stand a chance (*v. para 3*)
4 standing (*n. para 5*)
5 it stands to reason (*phr. para 3*)
6 standard (*n. para 1*)
7 stand out (*v. para 1*)
8 outstanding (*adj. para 1*)

a) to be in a situation that makes something likely to happen for you
b) according to the way a person views a situation
c) to be easily noticed or very obvious
d) an acceptable level of quality or achievement
e) to have the possibility of doing something
f) extremely good or impressive
g) someone's success or status
h) it is the logical conclusion

C VOCABULARY: WORDS RELATED TO *STAND* Work in groups. Discuss the questions.

1 What information in the text stood out to you as surprising or especially interesting?
2 In your country, do you stand a chance of getting a good job just on the basis of a degree from a college of good standing, or are hiring standards changing?
3 In your opinion, what qualities make someone an outstanding job candidate?

7 WRITING: sentence variety — punctuation with connectors

If you use only simple sentences, even if they are grammatically correct, your writing will not sound sophisticated. Combining ideas results in different sentence types. In order to do this successfully, you need to know the punctuation rules for different types of connectors.

A Read the excerpt from a personal essay from a college application. Underline the connectors that join ideas, such as *but*, *so*, *although*, *when*, and *however*.

PERSONAL ESSAYS

1. Describe your intellectual interests, their evolution, and what makes them exciting to you.

Last summer I traveled in Turkey, where I first experienced how cultural customs affect the way people do business. While browsing the bazaars, I quickly noticed that most purchases required bargaining. Sometimes I pretended not to be interested in a product, even though I actually wanted to buy it, and I often got a better price this way. However, I always had the feeling that I wasn't getting the best price. Turkish and American prices differ wildly, so I had no reliable standard of comparison. I eventually realized there is no "real price"; that is, the price is only what the seller will accept and what the buyer will give at any given moment. Since what is acceptable to both buyer and seller depends on the circumstances, the price is always different.

B Look at the underlined words in Exercise A. Choose the correct options to complete the punctuation rules.

1 Use a *comma* / *semicolon* before words like *and*, *but*, *or*, and *so*.
2 Use a *period* / *comma* before connectors like *because*, *where*, and *even though* when they appear in the middle of a sentence.
3 Use a *comma* / *semicolon* before words like *however*, *that is*, and *on the other hand* when they appear in the middle of a sentence. *Use* / *Don't use* a comma after these words.
4 *Use* / *Don't use* a comma after words like *however* and *therefore* at the beginning of a sentence.
5 When words like *since* and *because* appear at the beginning of a sentence, use a *comma* / *period* at the end of the clause, not after the word.

C Combine the two ideas into one sentence using the connector in parentheses and the correct punctuation.

1 Cross-country running is a compelling activity for me. It is one of the purest forms of effort. (*because*)
____

2 I train hard all year. I truly learned what "trying hard" meant when our team ran up Bear Lake Mountain. (*however*) ________________
____

3 Our coach challenged the team to run up the mountain without walking. I decided to take the challenge. I wasn't a top runner on the team. (*although*) ________________
____

4 Sometimes I felt like quitting. My teammates encouraged me. (*but*) ________________
____

5 We were almost at the top. All my teammates quit and walked. (*when*) ________________
____

6 My coach wouldn't know if I walked. I would know. (*but*) ________________
____

7 I didn't quit. I didn't want to let myself down. (*because*) ________________
____

lifeSkills

ANTICIPATING CULTURAL DIFFERENCES

- Decide what information you might need to know.
- Consider possible difficulties caused by cultural differences.
- Figure out how and where to get the information you need.

A Read the information from AIESEC, a global student-run organization. Then imagine you are planning to apply for an internship in Cameroon. Complete the chart with some questions about the culture that you would like answered before you go.

PERSONAL & PROFESSIONAL CHALLENGE IN A GLOBAL ENVIRONMENT

The Global Internship Program gives students and recent graduates the opportunity to take on a cross-cultural professional development experience with leading global brands and small to medium sized enterprises in 125+ countries and territories. The Programme specifically targets skill development both to meet the education plan of the intern participating as well as to support filling a talent need for the company.

Details:

- Duration: 6 weeks to 18 months
- Salary covers living costs except some development internships
- It takes between 2–7 months to find an internship and complete the selection process
- Application fee varies by country
- Airfare is usually not included

Clothing	Food	Time
· Do interns dress formally or informally? · ______	· What time of day is the main meal eaten? · ______	· Do meetings usually start on time? · ______
Gifts	**Making friends**	**Other**
· What are some appropriate gifts to bring from my country? · ______	· Do men and women socialize together? · ______	· ______ · ______

B **Read this blog entry from a previous intern. Then discuss the questions with a partner.**

PRINT | LIKE IT (16) | COMMENT (5) | EMAIL

July 28

The Center here offers a range of trips, so I decided to climb Mt. Cameroon with some of the other interns. We had a three-day weekend recently, and I wasn't sure I'd get another chance. But I almost thought we wouldn't make it! We set a time with the bus driver the day before—8:00 am. At 9:15, I went to the driver's house to get him. Finally we were all on the bus, but we still faced more delays. First the driver needed to buy gas. Why didn't he do that yesterday? Then at the gas station he started talking with friends. Come on! If he stopped to chat with whoever he met, we'd never get there. One of the other interns helped me relax, though. She reminded me that socializing is an essential part of Cameroon's culture. Friends and relationships are so important here. It stands to reason that if you run into someone you know, you'll spend time talking with him. I value my friends too, but sometimes when faced with work or school, I ignore them. And you know what? We got there in plenty of time, and Mt. Cameroon was outstanding. Click here for my hiking photos.

1 What difficulty did the intern have?
2 What caused this difficulty?
3 What values do you imagine are common in the intern's home country that are different in Cameroon?
4 What information could the intern have researched before his internship that would have prepared him for this situation?

C **Work in pairs. Look at the sources and think about what kind of information they provide. Then compare with your list of questions from Exercise A. Where would you go to find the information to answer your questions?**

- the website of the internship organization
- a citizen of Cameroon
- a former intern from your own country
- a guide book
- a travel agency
- an online blog by a foreign tourist visiting Cameroon
- a news article about current events in Cameroon
- the Embassy of Cameroon in your own country

D **Discuss the questions.**

1 Look back at the questions you wrote in Exercise A. Which ones are relevant for a visitor to your country? How would you answer them?
2 What other cultural information about your country do you think would be important for a visitor to know?

REFLECT ... How can the skill of anticipating cultural differences be useful to you in **Work & Career** and **Study & Learning**?

HOW TO SAY IT

It's not that common for ... to ...
It's normal to ...
They'd need to know that whenever we ...
If they don't want to stand out too much, they'd have to ...

RESEARCH ...

Choose an upcoming event or decision in your life such as a job, internship, vacation, or new course for which you will need information in advance. Prepare a list of questions for which you want answers. Decide where you will go to find the answers, and then conduct your research. Report back to the class about the process.

Language wrap-up

1 VOCABULARY

Complete the paragraph with appropriate forms of the words and phrases from the box. (10 points)

a broad range of | be faced with | drop out of | get a college degree | outstanding | set goals | stand a chance | stand to reason | standing | take into account

For many students, (1) ________________ means not only studying hard, but also (2) ________________ high tuition fees, which necessitate getting a job. Students often work long hours, which can obviously affect their grades and academic (3) ________________ if they don't have enough time to study. Sadly, many students end up (4) ________________ college, and those students often don't (5) ________________ of getting a high-level job. However, many universities offer work-study programs with (6) ________________ on-campus jobs that can help a student pay tuition fees. Unlike so many off-campus jobs, work–study programs (7) ________________ the fact that students need plenty of time to study. It (8) ________________ that students in these programs are often able to maintain an (9) ________________ grade point average even though they have to work. Of course, combining work with going to school requires the ability to be organized and to (10) ________________, but work-study programs can make that just a little bit easier for students.

8–10 correct: I can use specific verb collocations and words related to *stand*.
0–7 correct: Look again at Sections 1 and 6 on pages 46 and 50. SCORE: /10

2 GRAMMAR

A Complete the paragraph with *however*, *whatever*, *wherever*, *whenever*, or *whoever*. (6 points)

I've decided to hire a personal tutor to help me with my chemistry class. (1) ________________ I listen to my professor's lectures, I feel confused. Reading the textbook doesn't help, and (2) ________________ wrote it doesn't explain things very well. I've reread my notes, looked up explanations online, and studied with my roommate, but (3) ________________ I've tried hasn't worked for me, so it's time to try something new. I've also decided to do my homework alone instead of with friends because (4) ________________ my friends are, they are listening to music! It's very distracting. I'm ready to try new methods of learning, too. I will study (5) ________________ my tutor asks me to. (6) ________________ said chemistry was the hardest class at this college wasn't kidding!

B Combine the sentence pairs to make mixed conditional sentences. (4 points)

1 Your friend had to start working after high school. He doesn't have a college degree.
____

2 Your college has a high standing. You got a good job after you graduated.
____

3 Your colleague didn't understand the instructions. He is writing his report again.
____

4 Your boss doesn't have good communication skills. She made people angry yesterday.
____

8–10 correct: I can use relative pronouns with *–ever* and mixed conditionals.
0–7 correct: Look again at Sections 2 and 5 on pages 47 and 49. SCORE: /10

SPEAKING WORKSHOP

Expressing and supporting personal preferences

A 1.22 **Listen to someone answering the question in the box. Note the reasons she gives. Compare your notes with a partner.**

Would you rather take a class entirely online, or in a traditional classroom setting?

B Listen again. Complete the sentences.

1 I ______________________ take a class in a traditional classroom setting ______________________ an online class.
2 ______________________ main reasons.
3 The first ______________________ I'm just not very good with technology.
4 ______________________, I forget my password, lose my student ID, click on the wrong link …
5 ______________________ is that I work better in small groups.
6 ______________________, I don't do very well without supervision.
7 That's why an online class really ______________________.

C Complete the outline to give your answer to the question.

Preference: ______________________
Reason 1: ______________________
Example: ______________________
Reason 2: ______________________
Example: ______________________
Reason 3: ______________________
Example: ______________________

D Talk to your group or to the whole class and answer the question in Exercise A.

HOW ARE YOU DOING?

- ◯ I clearly stated my preference.
- ◯ I gave reasons to explain my preference.
- ◯ I used examples to support my reasons.

UNIT 5 ON THE WILD SIDE

IN THIS UNIT YOU

- learn language to talk about animals and conservation efforts
- read a magazine article about the interdependency of species
- talk about animal protection and rescue
- listen to a story about an orangutan
- write a letter to a newspaper editor about an animal welfare / conservation issue
- learn about decision-making styles
- watch a video about suburban beekeeping

READING
understanding definitions

Sometimes writers give definitions of words directly in a text. Why might they do this?

SPEAKING
summarizing

In what situations to you have to give an oral summary? What are some different types of information you might summarize?

LIFE SKILLS
SELF & SOCIETY

understanding decision-making styles

When you are a member of a group, do you prefer to take part in making decisions, or to have someone else make them?

A Draw at least three arrows between the parts of the ecosystem that you consider to be directly connected in some way. Then explain to a partner why you have drawn the arrows.

For example:
You could draw an arrow going from the fish to the heron because fish are a food source for birds.

A: *I think … and … are linked because …*
B: *I've drawn this arrow because …*

B Work in groups. Discuss how the things in the pictures can affect people.

Trees reduce air pollution by taking in carbon dioxide and releasing oxygen.

1 GRAMMAR: impersonal passive

A LANGUAGE IN CONTEXT Read the article. Which opinion about bats is closest to your own?

NOTICE!

Underline the passive verbs. Circle the subjects. What two different verb forms do you notice?

Bats about Bats

It is said that beauty is in the eye of the beholder, meaning that what's beautiful to one person might look unappealing to another. Not only is beauty individual, it is also cultural. One fascinating example of this is the bat. In Western Europe and North America, bats are thought to be scary or even dangerous. People think of the legends of vampires, or of diseases that can be spread by bats. Even in areas where it is known that bats pollinate plants and eat harmful insects such as mosquitoes, most people would say they find bats ugly. In China, on the other hand, it is believed that bats bring luck. The word for "bat" in Chinese sounds the same as the word for happiness, and bats have therefore come to represent happiness and good fortune. Because bats have a long lifespan, they can also symbolize longevity. Bat images can frequently be found in Chinese art. So whether a particular animal is considered friend or foe might just depend on where you live!

B ANALYZE Read the article in Exercise A again.

Form Complete the table with examples from the article.

Active	Impersonal passive 1: *It* + passive + *that* clause	Impersonal passive 2: subject + passive + infinitive
People say that beauty is in the eye of the beholder.	It is said that beauty is in the eye of the beholder.	Beauty is said to be in the eye of the beholder.
People think that bats are scary.	It is thought that bats are scary.	(1) __________ scary.
People know that bats pollinate plants.	(2) __________ bats pollinate plants.	Bats are known to pollinate plants.
People believe that bats bring luck.	(3) __________ bats bring luck.	Bats are believed to bring luck.

Common verbs used with the impersonal passive include *assume, believe, claim, consider, estimate, know, recommend, report, say, think*, and *understand*.

Function Choose the correct option to complete each sentence.

1 The impersonal passive is more *formal / informal* than the active.
2 The impersonal passive is *more / less* common than the active.
3 We use the impersonal passive with *active verbs / reporting and opinion* verbs.

C PRACTICE Rewrite the sentences in two different ways using the impersonal passive.

1 In ancient Egypt, people believed that beetles were lucky.
2 People in Greece think that bulls represent strength.
3 Deer are often shown in Chinese art because people say they symbolize prosperity.
4 Many people think that elephants have a good memory.
5 Some cultures believe that goldfish bring good luck to marriages.
6 Where I grew up, many people thought that black cats were unlucky.

D NOW YOU DO IT Work in groups. Discuss the questions.

Talk about common beliefs in your culture. What animals have the most positive associations? What animals are generally considered unlucky or dangerous?

2 LISTENING: to a story

A Read the synopsis from a radio show guide. What do you think probably happens in the story?

DECEMBER 8, 9:00 A.M.

THE ANIMAL HOUR

Writer Margaret Nelson reads a short story called *Lena*, from her collection of stories about animals. Nelson is active in several animal rescue programs, and last year she traveled to the island of Borneo to visit an orangutan sanctuary. This story is based on the life of an orangutan named Lena. This is not just another feel-good animal story with a happy ending; Nelson hopes that people will listen not only to the story, but also to the messages within it.

B VOCABULARY: ANIMAL RESCUE Read sentences (a–f) from the story *Lena*. Write the words in bold next to their definitions (1–6).

a) Lena's **natural habitat**, the Indonesian rainforest, is being destroyed at a frightening speed, and over half of the rainforest has already been destroyed.
b) Humans helped the young apes learn essential orangutan skills that they would have learned from their mothers if they had not been raised **in captivity**.
c) In **the wild**, young orangutans stay with their mothers for eight years.
d) Today, orangutans are an **endangered species**.
e) On the day of their **release**, they were taken deep into the forest.
f) **Smugglers** sell the young apes to people who don't care that these animals are not meant to be pets.

1 ________________: a situation in which wild animals are kept by people
2 ________________: a place where humans do not live
3 ________________: a type of animal or plant that may soon become extinct
4 ________________: the act of letting an animal leave the place where you have been keeping it
5 ________________: people who take things into or out of a country illegally to earn money
6 ________________: a specific environment where a species typically originates from

C 1.23 **VOCABULARY: ANIMAL RESCUE** Listen to the story. Take notes to help you remember the important points. Then use the words in Exercise B to help you summarize the story with a partner.

D Work in pairs. Discuss the questions. Use information from the story and your own ideas.

1 Why are orangutans becoming an endangered species?
2 Why do you think it often takes several years before orangutans can be released back to their natural habitat?
3 In your opinion, does it really matter if an animal becomes extinct? Why or why not?

3 GRAMMAR: passive modals

A 1.24 **LANGUAGE IN CONTEXT** **Listen to the conversation. What do Lee and Larissa agree about? What do they disagree about?**

Lee: We can take a walk by the lake. I think the zoo has been closed for repairs.

Larissa: No, wait—the gates are open, so <u>it can't have been closed</u> yet. Let's go in!

Lee: Actually, I'd rather not. I don't like zoos because wild animals shouldn't be kept in captivity. In fact, I think zoos <u>ought to be banned</u>.

Larissa: Really? I disagree. A lot of good things can be done at zoos. For example, some species may have been saved from extinction because of zoo breeding programs.

Lee: Well, endangered species could be bred anyway and then released into their natural habitats.

Larissa: But their natural habitat may have been destroyed. Where would they be released?

Lee: True. People shouldn't have been allowed to destroy those habitats. We need stronger laws to stop that from happening.

NOTICE!

Look at the underlined phrases. What form of the verb follows the word ***be***?

B ANALYZE **Read the conversation in Exercise A again.**

Form & Function **Complete the table with examples from the conversation.**

Modal	Form	Function	Examples
can, could, may, might, will, would	modal verb + *be* + past participle	We use these forms to talk about present and past ability or future possibility in the passive.	*Endangered species* (1) ______________ *anyway.* *I disagree. A lot of good things* (2) ______________ *at zoos.* *Where* (3) ______________ *they* ______________?
must, ought to, should	modal verb + *be* + past participle	We use these forms to talk about necessity and advisability in the passive.	*... wild animals* (4) ______________ *in captivity.* *In fact, I think zoos* (5) ______________.
could, can't may, might, must	modal verb + *be / have been* + past participle	We use these forms to talk about deduction and speculation in the present or past.	*The gates are open so it* (6) ______________ *yet.* *Some species* (7) ______________ *from extinction.*
should	modal verb + *have been* + past participle	We use this form to give criticism of something that happened in the past.	*People* (8) ______________ *to destroy those habitats.*

C PRACTICE **Complete the paragraph from a wildlife conservation blog. Use active or passive forms of the verbs in parentheses.**

Supporters of zoos ought to (1) ______________ (*visit*) zoos more often. If they spent more time observing zoo animals, they might (2) ______________ (*realize*) that wild animals shouldn't (3) ______________ (*keep*) in captivity. Zoo proponents argue that animals bred in zoos can (4) ______________ (*use*) to increase wild populations and that these breeding programs can (5) ______________ (*save*) species from extinction. However, the responsibility for the survival of wildlife cannot (6) ______________ (*give*) to zoos. Governments must (7) ______________ (*hold*) responsible for the well-being of the planet. Too often, politicians promise that the environment will (8) ______________ (*protect*), but this does not happen. Many species that are now extinct could (9) ______________ (*save*) if governments had acted responsibly at the time. The public must (10) ______________ (*demand*) action from their elected officials. Act now!

WATCH OUT!

✘ Their habitats shouldn't have destroyed.

✓ Their habitats shouldn't have been destroyed.

D NOW YOU DO IT **Work in groups. Discuss whether you agree or disagree with the ideas in Exercise C.**

4 PRONUNCIATION: final consonant clusters

A 1.25 Listen to the words and notice the sounds in the consonant clusters in bold. Then listen again and practice the words.

Two final consonant sounds: hi**ves**, pa**ths**, pe**st**, expe**ct**, wi**dth**, le**ngth**, wa**tched**
Three final consonant sounds: abso**rbed**, u**rged**, swa**rmed**, wa**rned**, invo**lved**, ta**stes**, ma**sks**, ri**sks**

B 1.26 Listen to the text. Work in pairs and practice reading it, paying attention to the consonant clusters.

We were absorbed as we watched the men in safety masks approach the bee hives. The bees swarmed the length of the paths to the hives as their instincts urged them to attack. We were warned of the risks involved in watching, but we wanted to find out what fresh honey tastes like!

5 SPEAKING: summarizing

To give an oral summary of a text, identify the main ideas, select a few key words, decide on the clearest order for presenting them to your listener, and then explain the main ideas in your own words.

A Work in pairs. Read the question. Student A, read Jake509's answer. Student B, read Diane_Flint's answer. Decide whether each writer is for or against the sale of wild species as pets.

Animal Issues

Home Account Login

Do you think pet stores should be allowed to sell wild species as pets?

Jake509: If pet stores are not allowed to sell wild species, wild animals will be bought from smugglers or other illegal sources. However, if people buy animals in pet stores, and if pet stores buy from authorized breeders, the illegal capture and sale of wild animals can be stopped, or at least reduced. It is also a fact that some pet stores help educate people about animals, both domestic and wild. Anyone who buys an animal at a good store will be given detailed instructions for taking care of it. When people have some contact with wild animals, they are much more likely to support efforts to preserve habitats and save endangered species.

Answer

Diane_Flint: I know that most of the wild animals sold in pet stores are bred in captivity, and in most cases these animals could never be released into the wild, but that does not mean that they make good pets. Many people buy cute baby animals and then do not know what to do with them when they grow up and begin to exhibit behaviors like biting or scratching. Furthermore, many animals are still caught in the wild, which damages wild populations and causes trauma and suffering for the animals that are caught. These factors should be considered by anyone who is thinking of buying a wild animal as a pet.

B Prepare to summarize the answer you read in Exercise A. Underline the main ideas in the answer you read in Exercise A. Then answer the questions.

1 What is the writer's thesis, or most important point?
2 Can you state the main ideas you underlined in your own words?
3 Should any details or examples be included in your summary?
4 Choose 3–5 key words to use in your summary.

C Work in pairs. Give your partner a summary of the answer you read. Then discuss which point of view you agree with.

6 WRITING: a letter to a newspaper editor

A What are some reasons for protecting these creatures? What are some reasons for getting rid of them?

1 deer 2 mosquitoes 3 wolves

B Read the letter at the bottom of the page. Summarize the main argument in one sentence.

C VOCABULARY: ADVERB-ADJECTIVE COLLOCATIONS Match the adverbs with the words that they are commonly used with.

1	over/under	a)	organized/effective/successful
2	highly	b)	populated/estimated/utilized
3	well/badly/poorly	c)	organized/done/thought-out

D VOCABULARY: ADVERB-ADJECTIVE COLLOCATIONS Write the correct collocations from Exercise C next to the concepts from the letter below.

1 bow hunting ____________________
2 effort needed from both people and the government ____________________
3 the area ____________________

E Work in pairs. Use the guidelines and example to write a letter to the editor stating your opinion. Include at least one phrase from each group in Exercise C.

1 Choose one of these topics:
   - Animals in captivity in zoos
   - The sale of wild animals as pets
   - The control of "suburban wildlife" such as deer or squirrels
2 State your opinion in a topic sentence.
3 Briefly explain the background to the problem.
4 State your arguments/opinions.
5 Write a concluding sentence which re-states your topic sentence in different words.

The Morning Gazette

Monday, April 16

Dear Environment Editor,

I am writing in the hope that I can motivate other people in our city to pressure the City Council to do something about our suburban deer. Although they are a native species, when humans settled in this area, they removed the wolves and other predators, without considering the effect that this would have on large mammals such as deer. With no animals to kill them off, the area is now overpopulated with deer, which poses a real threat to people. In some ways, they are just a nuisance—they eat the flowers out of our yards and trample our plants. But they also carry diseases that can be spread to humans through fleas and ticks. The most dangerous of these is Lyme disease, which can be fatal. Deer are also a significant problem on our roads. Did you know that last year, deer were blamed for 1.2 million car accidents in the U.S.A.? And they're not easy to get rid of. Some communities have turned to bow hunting to cope with their deer, but this method hasn't been highly successful, and it isn't safe for people. It will take a well-organized effort from both private citizens and the city government to combat the suburban deer.

Scott Stewart, Cool Springs

7 READING: understanding definitions

Being able to recognize definitions helps you to understand both concepts and specific words in a text. Definitions may be given directly, signaled by punctuation, or implied by a list of examples.

A Work in pairs. Discuss the questions.

1 When is the last time you saw a bee? Where did you see it, and what was it doing?
2 How do you think bees can have an effect on our lives?
3 Skim the article. Where do you think you might see an article like this?

B Read the article and discuss the questions in groups.

1 What problem does the article discuss? Why is it an important problem?
2 What causes of the problem are mentioned? Can you think of any others?
3 What solutions does the article propose? Can you think of any other solutions?

The Buzz about Bees

[1]If the price of food is higher next year, don't blame your supermarket—blame the death of millions of beehives, a phenomenon known as colony collapse disorder, or CCD. In fact, CCD has destroyed more than 10 million beehives since 2007 just in North America. Each colony, or community, of honeybees, contains around 30,000–50,000 insects, so the number of insect fatalities is enormous.

[2]There are known to be around 20,000 different species of bees, which live on all continents except Antarctica. Bees of all types are pollinators—that is, by spreading pollen when they fly from flower to flower, they fertilize plants, which causes fruits or vegetables to grow. Many North American crops, including apples, apricots, blackberries, carrots, almonds, broccoli, onions, watermelon, and more, cannot be fertilized except by bees. Fewer bees, therefore, means fewer (and more expensive) apples; no bees means no apples.

[3]It is now understood that CCD has more than one cause. Originally, it was thought that pesticides—chemicals sprayed on crops to kill insects—were responsible for killing the bees. However, CCD was observed among bees in the wild who fed from wildflowers as well as those which pollinated commercial crops. In the 1980s, varroa mites, which are parasites that suck blood from both adult and developing honeybees, were introduced into the southern United States. and they have spread from there. Loss of habitat is another problem for bees. Human development has resulted in a loss of plants that produce food for bees and a loss of space for them to build their hives in peace. It is even thought that climate change is stressing bee health.

[4]The real cause of the bees' decline is probably a combination of all these factors. It has been shown that pesticides and fungicides, used to kill funguses on food crops, don't necessarily kill bees, but they do weaken them—which leaves them more vulnerable to diseases and mites.

[5]While there are products such as Apistan, which can kill varroa mites, they are not highly effective. A better solution must be found, including protection of bees' natural habitat and a reduction or elimination of agricultural chemicals that weaken and kill bees. For both ecological and economic reasons, we simply can't afford to lose our honeybees.

C Read the article again. Match the term being defined (1–6), the method of definition (a–f), and the definition (i–vi). The first one is done for you.

1 colony collapse disorder	a) *that is*	i. chemicals that kill insects
2 colony	b) a list of examples	ii. community
3 pollinators	c) *which* + explanation	iii. the death of millions of beehives
4 crops	d) or	iv. plants grown for food
5 pesticides	e) definition between dashes [—]	v. something that fertilizes plants by spreading pollen
6 varroa mites	f) *known as*	vi. parasites

lifeSkills

UNDERSTANDING DECISION-MAKING STYLES

- Understand the advantages and disadvantages of different decision-making styles.
- Determine which decision-making style is most appropriate for a given situation.
- Carry out the decision-making process, and reflect on whether it went well.

A **Work in pairs and discuss the questions.**

1 Do you find it easier to make decisions on your own, or as part of a group?
2 What kind of problems can arise when making decisions as a group?

B **Write a word or phrase from the box next to each description of a decision-making style.**

authoritarian   committee   consensus   majority rule

1 ________________: The decision is made by holding a vote on two or more options. Each person gets one vote, and the option that receives the most votes wins.
2 ________________: In a large organization or group, people choose a smaller group of people to make the decision. The large group agrees to accept the decision made by the smaller group.
3 ________________: One person makes the decision for the whole group.
4 ________________: The aim is that everyone in the group should agree on the final decision. If there are different opinions, people talk and compromise until disagreements are resolved.

C **Check the statements that you think apply to each decision-making style. (In some cases, you can check more than one statement.) Discuss your answers with a partner.**

	Authoritarian	Committee	Consensus	Majority rule
a) It's a slower method.				
b) It's a faster method.				
c) Everyone's opinion is heard.				
d) It's fair to everyone.				
e) Power is not equal.				
f) It's a good way of making decisions about how a country is run.				
g) It's a good way of making decisions in a small organization.				

Self and Society
Work and Career
Study and Learning

D Work in pairs. Discuss which decision-making style you would recommend in each situation. Explain why.

1 A family—parents and two children—are discussing whether to get a pet.
2 The family has decided to get a pet and they are deciding what kind of pet to get.
3 A zoo needs to hire a new veterinarian.
4 There is a proposal to turn a large city park into an open-air arts and crafts market.

E Work in groups of five (or another odd number). Read the biology assignment. Then follow the steps below.

BIO 101 • DUE: TUESDAY, APRIL 7

As we have discussed, we would like to motivate the school to get involved in animal welfare or environmental conservation. You have brainstormed ideas, and now a proposal has to be made to the school. Your group will evaluate the suggestions that have been made and will decide on one idea to present to the school. Each group will then explain to the class which idea they have chosen and why. The final decision on which idea to work up as a proposal will be decided on by class vote.

a) Get the school to join an international organization that works for the protection of endangered species and habitats in many different countries. Decide how money could be raised in your school and/or town to donate to the organization.
b) Start a campaign to educate students about ecology issues in your country. Encourage students to join reputable ecology groups in your country, either branches of international organizations or country-specific ones.
c) Start a responsible pet owner movement. Local vets can usually be persuaded to go to a school to talk about how to care for pets. Ask for volunteers to help in animal shelters and in finding homes for abandoned animals.

1 Individually, decide which idea you like best.
2 Then, tell your group which idea you like best.
3 As a group, choose a decision-making style that will best help you all agree on the same idea.

F Tell the class about your decision-making process.

- Which idea did your group choose?
- Which decision-making style did your group choose? Why?
- What was easy about that decision-making style? What was challenging?
- If you had to do it again, would you choose the same decision-making process? Why or why not?

HOW TO SAY IT

Some of us wanted to use the … method, but most wanted to use the … method, so we did.

The most/least popular/effective idea was …

We thought this method was highly / wasn't very effective because …

We probably overestimated/underestimated the difficulty of / time needed for this method.

The decision could have been made more easily using …

G Discuss the questions.

1 What have you learned about decision-making styles?
2 Which decision-making styles are you most likely to use for group decisions in the near future?

REFLECT … How can the skill of understanding decision-making styles be useful to you in **Work & Career** and **Study & Learning**?

RESEARCH …

Research the way laws are passed in your community, city, or country. (You may choose a specific example of a law, to narrow your focus.) Take notes on the process, and decide whether the process is mostly authoritarian, by committee, by consensus, majority rule, or a combination of styles. Report back to the class on the law-making process.

Language wrap-up

1 VOCABULARY

Complete the letter with the words and phrases from the box. (10 points)

effective endangered species in captivity highly natural habitat under released the wild thought-out underestimated

Dear Editor,

I believe that the Coldwater Wilderness Area, which is located not far from our city, is **(1)** ________________ -utilized and could be used in a number of different positive ways if the city had a well **(2)** ________________ plan for it. We have a highly **(3)** ________________ wildlife rescue program, and many of those rescued animals could be **(4)** ________________ into **(5)** ________________ in Coldwater instead of being given to zoos and kept **(6)** ________________ all their lives. Coldwater is a **(7)** ________________ for a number of **(8)** ________________, and the area could be used to help educate the public about environmental issues as well as provide recreation. I know that there is a **(9)** ________________ successful program at the zoo on local plants and animals, and maybe a trip to Coldwater could be included in their program. I feel strongly that the importance of educating people about our local resources cannot be **(10)** ________________. Why can't people have fun and learn at the same time?

Frederick Missen

8–10 correct: I can use words related to animal rescue, and adverb-adjective collocations.
0–7 correct: Look again at Sections 2 and 6 on pages 59 and 62. **SCORE:** /10

2 GRAMMAR

Complete the letter. Use the impersonal passive form of the verbs in parentheses and choose the correct modal structures. (10 points)

Dear Editor,

The Coldwater Wilderness Area **(1)** ________________ (said / be) our most beautiful natural park. For this reason, I am against the proposal to open up the lake to motorboats and the trails to snowmobiles in the winter. People **(2)** *should* / *shouldn't be* allowed to upset the natural environment for sports.
Currently, more than 15 species of fish **(3)** ________________ (think / live) in the lake. Those fish **(4)** *might be* / *might have been* killed if motorboats hadn't been banned. Let's not forget that this lake **(5)** ________________ (say / have) the best fishing in the state! That's another reason that motorboats **(6)** *ought to* / *might* be forbidden. The same goes for snowmobiles.
Did you know that the noise from snowmobiles **(7)** ________________ (believe / disturb) hibernating animals? For this reason alone, snowmobiles **(8)** *must* / *mustn't* be permitted. It **(9)** ________________ (say) that deer and other animals can be so frightened by the noise of snowmobiles that they injure themselves.
For these reasons, the Coldwater Wilderness Area **(10)** *must* / *might* be preserved as an area safe for both animals and people.

August Philips

8–10 correct: I can use the impersonal passive and passive modals.
0–7 correct: Look again at Sections 1 and 3 on pages 58 and 60. **SCORE:** /10

WRITING WORKSHOP

Writing a formal email request

A **Read the email asking the public for financial donations. What is the money needed for?**

Dear Community Supporter,

The Glenwood Raptor Center was created in 1987 to serve the needs of our area's wild birds of prey—eagles, owls, falcons, and more. Each year, we help rescue dozens of sick and injured birds. Our trained volunteer staff works to rehabilitate these birds so that they can be released back into the wild. We also conduct educational outreach programs to inform the public about the place these beautiful birds have in our environment, and how we can all work together to protect their habitat.

I'm writing to ask for a donation to our annual fund. Your gift helps pay for food and shelter for the birds, their medical expenses, our educational outreach programs in schools and community centers, and our nature center. A donation of just $50 includes an annual membership for the Glenwood Raptor Center, good for discounts on our gift shop items and free admission to any of our programs. For $100, you can sponsor an individual bird, for which you'll receive a photo of the bird, an adoption certificate, and regular updates about your sponsored bird's progress.

Click here to donate $50 or any amount of your choosing.

Thank you for your generosity.

Sincerely,

Judy McLaughlin

Community Outreach Director
Glenwood Raptor Center

B **Check the features that the email mentions.**

- ☐ the receiver's name
- ☐ the sender's name
- ☐ the pronoun *you*
- ☐ the pronouns *I* or *we*
- ☐ what the organization does
- ☐ how much money the organization currently has
- ☐ how much money the organization needs
- ☐ what the organization will spend money on
- ☐ a recommended amount to give

C **Look at the email again. Underline any phrases that could be used in any fundraising letter or email.**

D **Now write a formal campaign email asking for money for Greenvale Animal Shelter. Write at least two paragraphs, using the structure of the model in Exercise A. Write about 250 words.**

Greenvale Animal Shelter: cares for stray cats, dogs, rabbits, and other small animals. Finds homes for strays in the community. Reunites pet owners with lost pets. Educates public on how to care for pets. Needs money for food, blankets and bedding, veterinary care, pet supplies such as bowls and leashes, general office supplies, and educational programs. All workers are volunteers.

HOW ARE YOU DOING?

- ◯ I explained what the organization does.
- ◯ I directly asked for what my organization wants.
- ◯ I used a formal email format.

UNIT 6 MORE THAN MACHINES?

IN THIS UNIT YOU

- learn language to predict future developments
- listen to people giving their opinions on artificial intelligence
- write a summary of an article about robot capabilities
- read about the future of robots in the workplace
- talk about automation and robots
- learn about organizing an argument
- watch a video about how robotics can help disabled people

LISTENING

inferring opinions

People don't always give their opinion directly. In what situations might you not want to state your opinion openly and directly?

WRITING

summarizing

When might you be required to write a summary of something you've read? Would different situations require a different style? How?

LIFE SKILLS

STUDY & LEARNING

organizing an argument

To what extent do you agree with this statement? Explain your choice.

When you are putting forward an argument, your passion for what you believe is more important than how you organize your argument.

Strongly agree ○ Agree ○ Neither agree nor disagree ○ Disagree ○ Strongly disagree ○

A Work in pairs. Discuss the questions.

Do the pictures show machines or robots? What is the difference?
Which of the items in the pictures do you think is the most useful? Why?

1

2

3

4

5

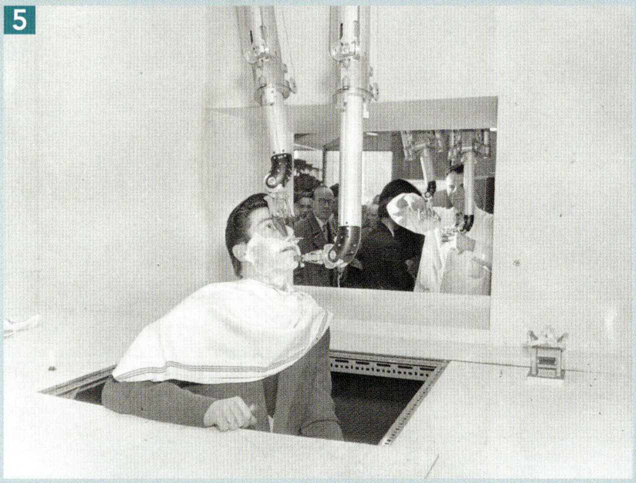

6

B Work in small groups. Discuss what tasks you think machines and/or robots will never be able to do. Give reasons.

1 GRAMMAR: future perfect

A LANGUAGE IN CONTEXT **Read the discussion board post. How does the writer think robots threaten our future?**

JULY 17

Who will have become obsolete in five years?

Hi, guys!

I saw something on TV about robots in the workplace last night, and it got me thinking. In five years' time, what will have changed? I know that some of you will have graduated by then and will have entered the world of work. Will some jobs have disappeared? Which ones? I know some won't have disappeared, but will have been fundamentally changed by robots and by automation. For example, doctors certainly won't have been replaced completely, but perhaps remote robots for surgery will have become the norm. I'd love to hear your comments on how you think the profession you're planning to follow will have changed in five years' time because of robots and automation!

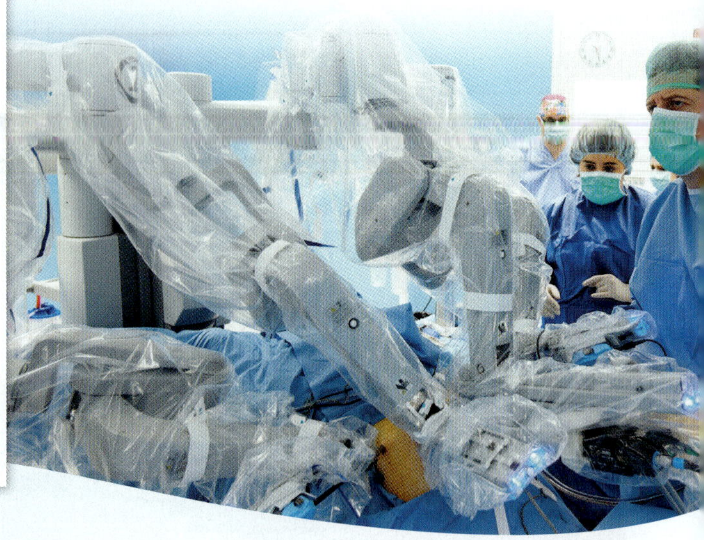

NOTICE!

Find an example of ***will*** and an example of ***won't*** in the text. What other words form the complete tense being used?

B ANALYZE **Read the post in Exercise A again.**

Form **Complete the table with examples from the text.**

Active or Passive	Form	Example
Active	*will/won't* + *have* + past participle	In five years' time, what **(1)** __________________? I know some **(2)** __________________ ...
Passive	*will/won't* + *have been* + past participle	... doctors certainly **(3)** __________________ completely ...

Function **Choose the correct option to complete the rule.**

The future perfect is used to describe an event that will be completed by ... a specific time in the future.

a) at *or* before **b)** after

WATCH OUT!

✘ By the year 2025, robots will become more common.

✓ By the year 2025, robots will have become more common.

C PRACTICE **Use the future perfect to combine the two ideas.**

1 15 years / robots become common around the home

____

2 the middle of this century / robots take over many manufacturing jobs in my country

____

3 four or five years / smartphones are replaced by smartwatches in some cases

____

4 another decade / the PC becomes obsolete

____

5 a few years / children don't ever see a telephone connected to the wall

____

6 the year 2050 / artificial intelligence isn't created

____

D NOW YOU DO IT **Work in pairs. Discuss your answers to the questions raised in the text in Exercise A. Then share your ideas with the whole class.**

2 SPEAKING: talking about automation

A 1.27 Listen to a man and a woman talking about an airplane missing its landing. Who blames automation and who blames the pilots? Which speaker do you agree with?

B VOCABULARY: PHRASES WITH ADJECTIVE + PREPOSITION
Listen again. Match the parts of the sentences. Check the meanings in a dictionary if necessary.

1 The pilots are **dependent**
2 They weren't **aware**
3 They should have been **focused**
4 It's too easy for them to be **distracted**
5 I'd be more **alarmed**
6 They're not going to be **overwhelmed**
7 I'm just **suspicious**

a) **by** emotions …
b) **on** them to control the plane.
c) **by** flying on a plane that wasn't automated.
d) **by** other things.
e) **of** too much automation.
f) **of** what was going on around them.
g) **on** what was happening!

C VOCABULARY: PHRASES WITH ADJECTIVE + PREPOSITION Work in pairs. Read the text and choose the correct expressions. With your partner, create a definition of *automation* in your own words.

[1]Automation is the use of control systems, along with information technology, to control machinery and processes. Many people are not **(1)** *aware of* / *alarmed by* what automation is, even as they and their lives become more **(2)** *distracted by* / *dependent on* automatic processes. A common mistake is to confuse it with mechanization. Mechanization provides humans with machines to assist with the muscular requirements of work. Machines do mechanical and repetitive work well because they don't get **(3)** *suspicious of* / *distracted by* thoughts or their environment. They work quickly and efficiently. However, automation is more than mechanical work. In automation, machines fulfill some human sensory and mental requirements as well.

[2]While automation reduces the need for human intervention further than mechanization, there are still some things that are beyond its scope. Human-level pattern and language recognition are still outside the capabilities of automated systems. Also, people are very good at dealing with situations that require understanding other people's behavior, which machines still cannot do. Finally, a well-trained human will not be **(4)** *overwhelmed by* / *distracted by* tasks that require subjective assessment.

[3]Despite these limitations, automation has had a huge impact on many industries and is used in a variety of ways, from automated telephone systems to transportation systems. Many people are **(5)** *suspicious of* / *aware of* automation, though. Skeptics are **(6)** *alarmed by* / *focused on* advances in automation and claim that automation is problematic because a machine cannot make the necessary judgments that a human can and cannot react to unusual or unforeseen circumstances. However, others argue that there is a place for automation alongside humans, doing tasks that are better suited to machines, while humans are **(7)** *focused on* / *distracted by* what they do best—working in situations that require subjectivity and judgment.

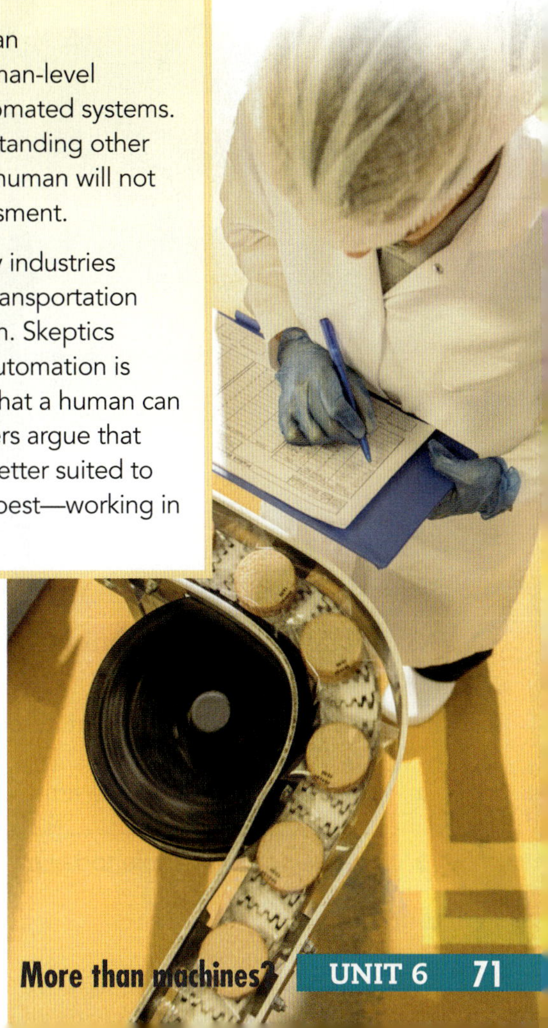

D Read the statement. Choose the option you agree with and plan a short presentation. Give reasons. Include examples of the types of automation you would include or eliminate.

We should *increase* / *decrease* the use of automation in planes and cars.

E Independent Speaking Work in pairs. Give a short presentation to your partner on your ideas about automation. Give examples.

3 READING: an online news article

A Read the article. According to the article, why do we not see "armies of robots" in the workplace?

DON'T EXPECT ROBOTS TO DO IT ALL FOR YOU —OR STEAL YOUR JOBS

Fay Schopen

[1]If you had walked into the Work Foundation's offices last week, at first glance everything would have looked normal. At the back of the reception area, however, on a large table, something strange **was going on**. Two robotic arms were in operation, the larger of the two sweeping slowly back and forth over a silicon block—an unlikely stand-in for a human body. This was a "robot assistant" for surgeons, designed to be a way to help them to find tumors. This technology could be in common use less than a decade from now.

[2]The demonstration was part of a debate at the Work Foundation about robots and enhanced humans, asking the question: will they steal our jobs? The answer, it seems, is "not quite." Geoff Mulgan, the chief executive of Nesta, a charity set up to promote innovation, **points out** that the situation where we see armies of robots in the workplace has yet to **come about**. Rather, globalization has left companies **going after** cheap labor overseas instead of replacing human beings with automatons.

[3]But technology *will* play a key part in the labor market of the future. A recent report forecasts a number of growth areas, particularly in professional and technical occupations, such as the digital sector, science, technology, engineering, and mathematics—the so-called STEM sector—construction, and automotive. Nevertheless, Neil Carberry, the director of employment and skills at a national business organization, notes that low-skilled work, such as cleaning or delivering goods, will also become higher skilled: "Workers will be using tools and IT to help them do a better job. They already use tablets or PDAs to help to manage their time." He argues, too, that traditional skills will continue be in demand. "More and more highly skilled work will **rely on** the capacity for judgment. Computers don't do that yet."

[4]So, if the workers of the future need to be good at using their judgment, at being in tune with their emotions and able to use technology with ease, how ready are we? The answer, perhaps, is to be both a STEM specialist and a generalist. "You will need to have a generic ability to **pick** things **up** quickly and refresh your education and learning throughout your whole life," Mark Beatson, the chief economist of the Chartered Institute of Personnel and Development, says. "The danger with specific skills is that they become redundant."

[5]And whatever you do, you'll be in it for the long haul. "Realistically, a lot of young people today will need to develop skills over 40 or 50 years of employment," according to Carberry. "They will need to be resilient."

Adapted from The Times online, http://www.thetimes.co.uk/tto/business/industries/technology/article3793519.ece

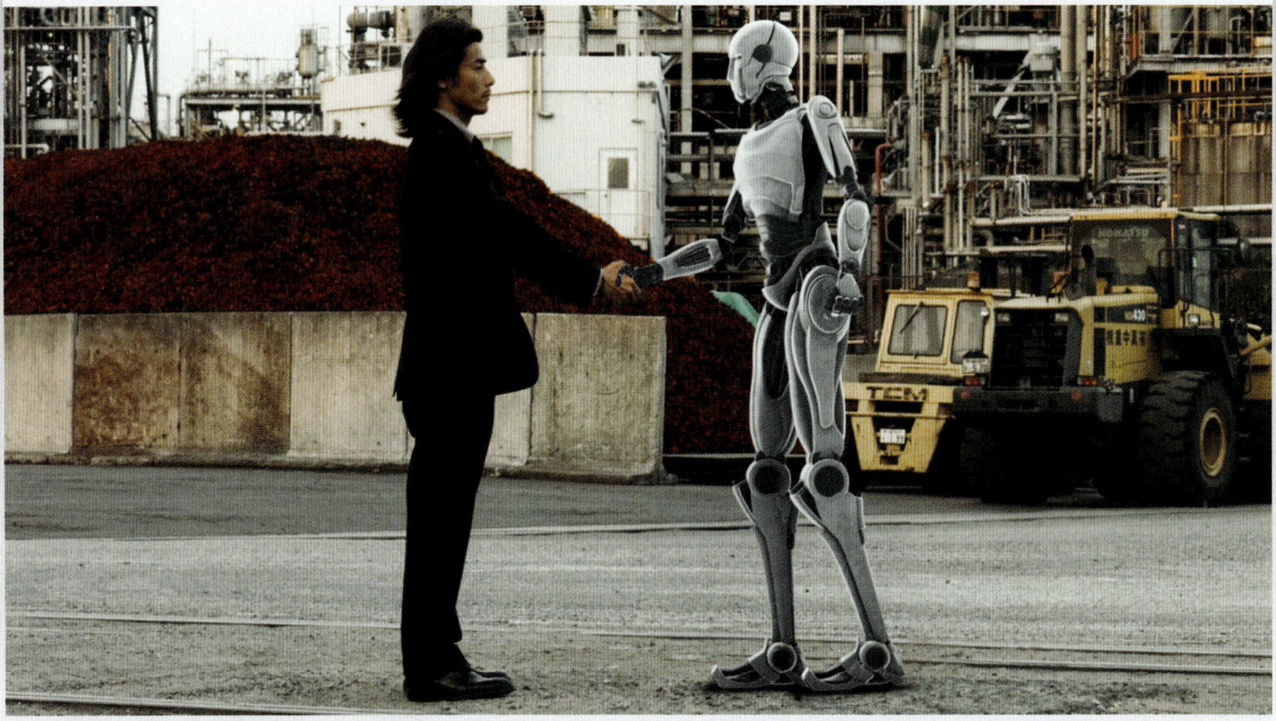

B Write one or two sentences in your own words to answer each of the questions.

1 What is the "robot assistant" used for?

______

2 What point is made in the article about low-skilled work?

______

3 Why will young people today need to be "resilient"?

______

C VOCABULARY: PHRASAL VERBS Look at the words in bold in the article on page 72. Study the context and suggest a definition for each phrasal verb. Check in a dictionary if necessary.

1 go on: ____________
2 point out: ____________
3 come about: ____________
4 go after: ____________
5 rely on: ____________
6 pick (something) up: ____________

D VOCABULARY: PHRASAL VERBS Complete this comment on the article. Use the phrasal verbs from Exercise C in the correct form.

Posted at 5:32 p.m. by Mechgirl85
I would like to **(1)** ____________ that it's all about what humans and robots each do best. Humans have a general ability to **(2)** ____________ skills, whereas robots have to be much more specialized. What's **(3)** ____________ in the world of work at the moment is this: manufacturers **(4)** ____________ robots to do the hard, physical work, while **(5)** ____________ people with the skills to manage other aspects of the business. This situation has **(6)** ____________ because of the different things that robots and people have to offer.

4 LISTENING: inferring opinions

Speakers don't always say what they mean in a direct way, especially if they are disagreeing with someone else. To understand a speaker's opinion, pay attention to tone of voice as well as word choice. The use of emphasis, for example, can indicate that the speaker means the opposite of what the words literally mean.

A 1.28 **Listen to a conversation about artificial intelligence (A.I.). Underline the best paraphrase of each sentence.**

1 Woman: Yeah, that'll happen.
   a) I think robots will be able to think one day. ___
   b) I don't think robots will be able to think one day. ___
2 Woman: Come on.
   a) I think your bread machine can think. ___
   b) I don't think your bread machine can think. ___
3 Woman: Would it?
   a) I think it would be wonderful. ___
   b) I don't think it would be wonderful. ___
4 Man: That's science fiction.
   a) I think it's possible. ___
   b) I don't think it's possible. ___
5 Man: OK, I see what you mean.
   a) I might be changing my mind. ___
   b) I totally agree with you. ___
6 Man: You're so serious tonight!
   a) You're very responsible. ___
   b) You should relax. ___

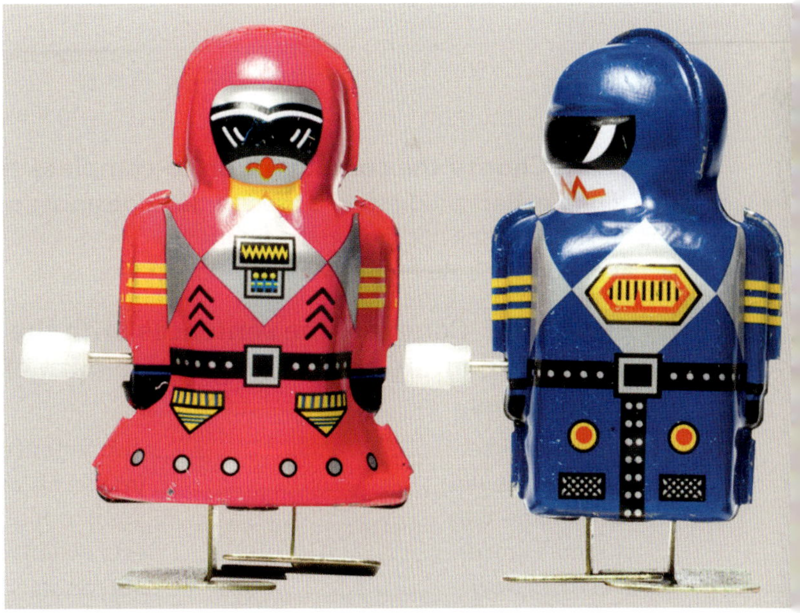

B Listen again. Note which of these options helped you understand the meaning of each statement. Write the correct letter(s) next to each part of the conversation in Exercise A.

A use of emphasis B word choice C tone of voice

C Work in groups. Discuss the questions.

1 Do you think it's possible to create a robot that is intelligent? Why or why not?
2 Do you think it's possible to create a robot that can feel emotions? Why or why not?
3 Would it be desirable to create an intelligent, feeling robot? Why or why not?

5 GRAMMAR: future perfect progressive

A LANGUAGE IN CONTEXT Read the blog post about robots of the future. Is the author's view positive, neutral, or negative? How do you know?

FUTURE THOUGHTS

JANUARY 27, BY HARRY WILLSON

Robots have already come to town, even if we're not always aware of it. Robots drill for our oil, drive and park our cars, and even have a part to play in medical operations. By the end of this year, in fact, I will have been using robots in my business for almost 20 years. And technology keeps on improving. Based on the advances I saw at the recent World Technology Fair, I can make these predictions about the use of robots in the long term:

- By the time I retire, people will have been living comfortably with robot pets, doctors, and other helpers for years.
- When my grandchildren are grown, engineers will have been making realistic-looking robots for so long that people won't be able to tell that they're actually robots filling the shoes of regular people.
- Before the end of this century, doctors will have been using robotic replacements for damaged organs in living beings for over 50 years.

NOTICE!
Find a form of the verb *live* and underline the complete tense, including all auxiliary words.

B ANALYZE Read the blog post in Exercise A again.

Form Complete the table with examples from the text.

Tense	Form	Example
Future perfect progressive	*will/won't* + *have* + *been* + *–ing* form	By the end of this year, in fact, I **(1)** ________ robots in my business for almost 20 years. When my grandchildren are grown, engineers **(2)** ________ realistic-looking robots for so long that …

Function Choose the correct option to complete the rule.
The future perfect progressive is used to describe an action or situation happening … a specific time in the future.
a) at a moment before   b) for a period of time up to

WATCH OUT!
✘ By the time I get there, my friend will be waiting for two hours.
✓ By the time I get there, my friend will have been waiting for two hours.

C PRACTICE Complete the sentences with the simple present or the future perfect progressive form of the verb in parentheses.

1 By dinner time, I ________ (*work*) for seven hours with no break.
2 By June, Steven ________ (*make*) his own robots for four years.
3 By the time they ________ (*get*) to high school, students (*take*) ________ tests online for several years.
4 That company ________ (*use*) robots in all of their factories for over two years by 2018.
5 When he ________ (*retire*), my uncle ________ (*collect*) toy robots for more than half his life.
6 Mark ________ (*play*) that video game for a month by the time he ________ (*finish*) every level.

D NOW YOU DO IT Work in groups. Use the future perfect progressive to complete the sentences.

- By the time I am 30, …
- By the time I finish studying, …
- When I retire, …

6 PRONUNCIATION: linking words with a /w/ or a /j/ sound

A 1.29 **Listen to the phrases. Notice how the two words are joined with a /w/ or a /j/ sound.**

/w/	go on	no idea	two apples	true answer
/j/	I often	high altitude	we allow	he isn't

B 1.30 **Listen to the sentences. Then practice with a partner.**

1 If robots go on developing as they have been, I have no idea what it will lead to.
2 I often think that there'll be problems if we allow robots to become intelligent.

7 WRITING: summarizing

When writing a summary of a text, first identify the main ideas and the most important details. Then decide on the best order for the information and rewrite the ideas in your own words.

A Read the excerpt from an online article. Underline the main ideas. Circle the information to include in a summary (title, author, source, date).

SCIENCE FORUM

YOUR ONLINE SOURCE FOR BREAKING DEVELOPMENTS

Posted by Dr. Jake Helder, Robotics Department, NowTech Institute, on Jan. 8th, at 9:41 a.m. CST

ROBOTS: A NECESSARY EXPENDITURE

No one can deny that the past few years have seen some impressive developments in robotics, and the future looks even brighter for robot technology. My research is focused on using robots for search and rescue missions and environmental cleanups. For example, in the next few years, robots will have been developed that can instantly stop oil spills or radiation leaks, helping to prevent disasters like the 2010 oil spill in the Gulf of Mexico, or the 2011 leak at the Fukushima nuclear power plant in Japan. If government agencies continue to fund our research at current levels, robots will have started working on every continent except Antarctica by the end of this century, even if most people aren't even aware of their presence.

B Read the summaries of the excerpt. Which is the best summary? Why?

a) In an article for the online magazine *Science Forum* ("Robots: A necessary expenditure") on January 8, Dr. Jake Helder of NowTech Institute comments that continued funding of research will lead to more robots being developed and used. He predicts that in the future, more robots will be able to help with search and rescue missions and environmental cleanups in situations such as oil spills and radiation leaks.

b) An article, entitled "Robots: a necessary expenditure" appears in *Science Forum* (January 8) and talks about the uses of robots in the future. It is suggested that they will help stop oil spills and radiation leaks and therefore prevent environmental disasters. In the future, even though people might be unaware of their presence, robots will be working on every continent in the world except Antarctica.

C Read the excerpt from another article and write your own summary.

Posted by Laura Hayes, Ph.D., sociologist, on Jan. 9th, at 7:16 p.m. CST

ROBOTS OR PEOPLE: WHERE SHOULD OUR MONEY BE GOING?

Though robots definitely have their uses, I am concerned about investing much money into programs aimed at machines instead of people. Robots are enormously expensive. There will be a significant shortage of healthcare workers by the end of this decade — largely because of a lack of money. Robots can never replace trained personnel. Certainly they can play a key part in rescue efforts, for example, but robots can't make the kinds of independent decisions that people can; nor do they have the capacity to offer important emotional aid and support to victims. I'm concerned that those needs would be sacrificed if we continue to develop increasing numbers of machines for those situations.

D Work in groups. Compare your summaries. How are they similar? How are they different? Did you all include the same information?

lifeSkills

ORGANIZING AN ARGUMENT

- Choose an appropriate organizational pattern for your argument.
- Select points to include in your argument.
- Organize the points you want to make according to the pattern you have chosen.

A Complete the information about organizing an argument with the words and phrases from the box.

Context   Counter-arguments   Responses   Statement of your view   Supporting reasons

INTERNATIONAL COLLEGE: ACADEMIC SUPPORT SERVICE

During your time at International College, you will no doubt be asked to present arguments to your professor and to other students, both orally in seminars and in writing academic papers. It is important that you organize your arguments correctly to present the most convincing case for your point of view. The organizational pattern you choose may depend on the topic, but here is one option:

Provide context for your view, together with supporting reasons, and then look at counter-arguments (arguments against your view) and respond to them.

- **(1)** ______________ → This is a general introduction to the topic, giving some background information to introduce your point of view.
- **(2)** ______________ → This should be clear and specific, not just a general opinion. It should also be a view that someone could possibly argue against, not something that is obvious and that everyone accepts is true.
- **(3)** ______________ → These are what your view is based on. Present your reasons clearly and explain how they relate to your view. Add any further evidence or examples to support your view.
- **(4)** ______________ → These are points other people might make which suggest that your view is wrong. Use your imagination to think of the strongest arguments against your view.
- **(5)** ______________ → These are the reasons why the counter-arguments are incorrect. Show clearly why each counter-argument is wrong. If you can't think of a good response to a counter-argument, you may have to revise your view!

Contact the Academic Support Service for further guidance.

B As part of a course on technology, you are studying robots in the workplace. Your assignment is to present your views on one of these topics. Check the sentence that matches your view.

- ☐ In ten years' time, many people will have been made redundant as robots come to dominate in the workplace.
- ☐ In ten years' time, robots will have become common in the workplace, but humans will still have important roles in areas where robots lack skills.
- ☐ Putting robots in the workplace is expensive, and in ten years' time, little will have changed due to cheap human labor.

C Write three supporting reasons for the statement you have chosen. For each reason, add any further evidence or examples you can think of.

First reason:

Supporting evidence or examples:

Second reason:

Supporting evidence or examples:

Third reason:

Supporting evidence or examples:

D Write two counter-arguments that people might make against your view. Write your response to each counter-argument, explaining why it is wrong.

Example:
View: *In ten years' time, many people will have been made unemployed as robots come to dominate in the workplace.*
Counter-argument 1: Robots are too expensive to be widely used in the workplace.
My response: As robots become more common, they, and the computing power behind them, will become cheaper and cheaper.

Counter-argument 1:

My response:

Counter-argument 2:

My response:

E Make notes on what you plan to say in the introduction and the conclusion of your argument. Remember to follow the organizational pattern. Then present your argument to the class. Whose argument is the most convincing?

F Discuss the questions.

1 What have you learned about organizing an argument?
2 Did you feel that using the organizational pattern made your argument clearer and stronger?

HOW TO SAY IT

What I believe is …
One clear reason for this is …
Another fact that supports my view is …
Some may argue that …
However, in response to that, I would say that …

REFLECT … How can the skill of organizing an argument be useful to you in **Work & Career** and **Self & Society**?

RESEARCH …
Research robots in the workplace. Find information on some interesting developments. Make brief notes and report back to the class.

Language wrap-up

1 VOCABULARY

A Replace the words in parentheses with the words in the box and an appropriate preposition. You do not need to use all of the words. (6 points)

alarmed aware dependent distracted focused overwhelmed suspicious

A: Hey, are you **(1)** (*informed about*) ________________ the deadline for our robotics project?
B: Oh, yes, I know it's soon! I haven't been **(2)** (*paying attention to*) ________________ that project enough. I've been **(3)** (*much too busy with*) ________________ other work.
A: Well, our overall grade is **(4)** (*affected by*) ________________ it, so we really need to work on it this weekend. I'm **(5)** (*very worried about*) ________________ how much work there is left to do. Did you know that Andrew's team is already finished?
B: Oh, I'd be a little **(6)** (*doubtful*) ________________ anything Andrew says! Anyway, I'll be there on Saturday and we'll finish it off.

B Complete the sentences with an appropriate preposition. (6 points)

1 Young people these days can't rely ____________ following one career for the whole of their working lives.
2 I am thinking of going ____________ that part-time job available in the science lab.
3 Unemployment has come ____________ because of increased automation in the workplace.
4 It's important to point ____________ that technological progress creates both winners and losers.
5 A lot of interesting things are going ____________ in the world of robotics at the moment.
6 I find it quite easy to pick new things ____________, especially languages.

10–12 correct: I can use specific phrases with adjective + preposition and phrasal verbs.
0–9 correct: Look again at Sections 2 and 3 on pages 71, 72 and 73. **SCORE:** /12

2 GRAMMAR

Complete the sentences with the future perfect, the future perfect passive, or the future perfect progressive form of the verbs in parentheses. (12 points)

1 One week from now, I ______________________ (*buy*) my plane tickets.
2 By the time Kim starts her homework, I ______________________ (*finish*) mine.
3 By the time you finally get here, I ______________________ (*work*) for over three hours.
4 In another 10 years, scientists ______________________ (*invent*) robots that look just like real animals.
5 By tomorrow, it ______________________ (*rain*) for one whole week.
6 I ______________________ (*not finish*) this report by Friday.
7 Dan ______________________ (*date*) his girlfriend for exactly half a year in May.
8 By the time they finish high school, the students ______________________ (*write*) all of their in-class essays on laptops for over five years.
9 Before I graduate from college, I'm sure there ______________________ (*be*) another Mars landing.
10 Drive a different way. I don't think that accident on the highway ______________________ (*clear up*) yet.
11 Next April, Jenna and I ______________________ (*be*) married for ten years.
12 I can't pick you up on Saturday because my car ______________________ (*not repair*) by then.

10–12 correct: I can use the future perfect and the future perfect progressive.
0–9 correct: Look again at Sections 1 and 5 on pages 70 and 74. **SCORE:** /12

SPEAKING WORKSHOP Comparing and contrasting photographs

A 1.31 Read the question about the two photographs and listen to someone answering the question. Make notes of the speaker's main points. Then compare your notes with a partner.

What might working with robots be like in these situations?

B Listen again for phrases the speaker uses that mean the same as the phrases on the left. Write a word or short phrase in each blank.

1	It seems that the robots …	It ________ the robots …
2	My opinion is that …	I ________ that …
3	However, …	On the ________ …
4	I think it's possible that …	My ________ is that …
5	No doubt it's still …	________ it's still …
6	In contrast to the first situation …	________ the first situation …

C Prepare to present your answer to the question to the class. Make notes with your own ideas. Compare your ideas with a partner.

Photo A:	Photo B:
possibly boring and repetitive	*difficult, requires a lot of training*
________	________
________	________
________	________

D Present your ideas to the class.

HOW ARE YOU DOING?

- ◯ I briefly described what each photo shows.
- ◯ I gave my opinion clearly on working with robots in each situation.
- ◯ I compared and contrasted the two situations.

Communicative wrap-up
Units 1–2

1 FUNDRAISER

A Your class needs to raise money for a class trip. You have decided to have a yard sale. Think of two or three items that you can donate to the sale. Decide how much you think they are worth. Complete the table.

Item	Description	Sale price
(1)		
(2)		
(3)		

B Work in groups. Describe the items you will donate to the sale. Discuss whether or not you think each item will sell.

2 SPACE HOTEL

A Work in pairs. You are working for a hotel group that is planning to build a hotel in space. Discuss the questions and make notes. Add two questions of your own and then answer them.

1 Where in space will the hotel be located?
2 How will guests travel there?
3 What facilities will the hotel have?
4 What kind of activities will be offered?
5 When will the hotel be launched?
6 What kinds of public relations activities will inspire people to stay at the hotel?
7 ______
8 ______

B Join two other pairs to make a group. Take turns presenting your ideas. Explain why your hotel will be better than the hotels proposed by the other hotel groups.

3 CATEGORIES GAME

Work in groups. Follow the instructions to play the game.

- Choose one person to be the game host. The rest are players. The host will check the players' answers. If a player gives a correct answer, the host marks the question. If a player gives an incorrect answer, another player can answer.
- The players take turns answering questions. They can choose any question from any category that has not already been answered correctly. Each player reads the question aloud and answers. If the answer is correct, the player gets the number of points for that category.
- The host counts up the players' scores. The player with the most points wins.

DEFINITIONS
1 point

1 A person who can't do something is …
a) incapable.
b) insufficient.

2 Something that is not correct is …
a) immeasurable.
b) inaccurate.

3 To take something somewhere and leave it is to …
a) throw it in.
b) drop it off.

4 To pay for something with a good or a service instead of money is to …
a) barter.
b) consume.

5 When something is offered for free, it is …
a) second-hand.
b) up for grabs.

6 To present a new service or product is to … it.
a) launch
b) lobby

FACTS
2 points

1 What can you do on the website Freecycle?
a) buy cheap goods
b) swap one item for another
c) give away or get free items

2 What is the name of "freeconomist" Mark Boyle's first book?
a) *Freeconomics*
b) *The Moneyless Man*
c) *Barterrific*

3 Which TV show was the inspiration for the cell phone?
a) *Night Gallery*
b) *Star Trek*
c) *The Jetsons*
d) *Battlestar Galactica*
e) *The Twilight Zone*

4 Which figure represents the approximate age of the Earth?
a) 4.5 million years
b) 4.5 billion years

5 In what year was the first moon landing?
a) 1959
b) 1969
c) 1979
d) 1989

6 What technique from science fiction may be used by the British military in the future?
a) laser guns
b) invisible vehicles
c) electrical force fields

EXPLANATIONS
3 points

1 What is sustainable living?

2 What is a barter system?

3 How do websites like Freecycle and Barterrific help the environment?

4 Why do "freeconomists" believe it's better to live without money?

5 Why do some people believe it's likely that there is intelligent life on other planets?

6 Why are national space programs controversial?

SCORE YOURSELF!

Score 1–5 for the items below. Score 5 for things that are easy and 1 for things that are difficult.

I can describe objects and assess their monetary value.	5	4	3	2	1
I can talk about business and consumerism.	5	4	3	2	1
I can talk about space exploration.	5	4	3	2	1

If you gave yourself 1 or 2 for any of the statements, look at Units 1 and 2 again.

Communicative wrap-up
Units 3–4

1 ORDERING A STORY

Work in groups of six. Each group member chooses a different paragraph and studies the information. Then close your book, paraphrase the information, and tell it to your group. Finally, work as a group to put the paragraphs in order.

The Morris Worm

A Morris was quickly discovered to be the creator of the worm, and became the first person to be charged under the 1986 Computer Fraud and Abuse Act, a law that declared it illegal to hack into federal computers.

B Morris was a graduate student at Cornell University when he created the worm in 1988. He intended it to be harmless. However, he made a mistake in writing it, and it got out of hand, spreading much faster than he had anticipated.

C He had to pay a fine of $10,500 and perform 400 hours of community service, a sentence that even at the time was thought to be severe. Fortunately, his punishment did not decrease his interest in computers, and he has since had a successful career in the field.

D In fact, in just a few days, Morris' worm shut down one in ten computers connected by Arpanet (the predecessor of today's internet), infecting about 6,000 computers owned by universities, laboratories, and military and government offices. The overall damage was estimated to be between $100,000 and $10 million.

E What is an internet worm? Simply put, it's a computer program that is designed to copy itself and spread to other computers. They can be relatively harmless, and only take up a computer's space and resources, or they can be used to delete files or send email spam. And the Morris Worm was the first.

F Today, Robert Tappan Morris has a Ph.D. from Harvard University and is a tenured computer science professor at MIT. Twenty-five years ago, however, he was found guilty of a computer-related crime: creating the first-ever internet worm.

2 CHOICES

Work in pairs. Plan and practice a role-play of this discussion. Then present it to the class or another pair.

Student A:
You are a parent with no college degree. You feel that life would be easier now if you had gone to college.

Student B:
You are the son/daughter of Student A and you don't want to go to college. You think it would be better to get practical work experience.

A: *If I had gone to college, I might be a manager now.*
B: *I imagine so. But if you had become a manager, you might suffer from more stress now.*
A: *I suspect not. I would have more responsibility, and I'd like that.*

3 THE DISCUSSION CIRCLE

Work in small groups. Follow the instructions.

- Place a marker on START, and decide who will begin. Take turns. When it's your turn, roll a die and move the number of spaces indicated.
- Answer the question in the space you land on as completely as you can. Other players will ask you follow-up questions. When you have finished talking, hand the die to the next player.
- When another player is speaking, ask questions only. Don't give your own answers to that question.
- If you finish the questions, go back to the beginning and continue. If you land on the same question twice, roll the die again.

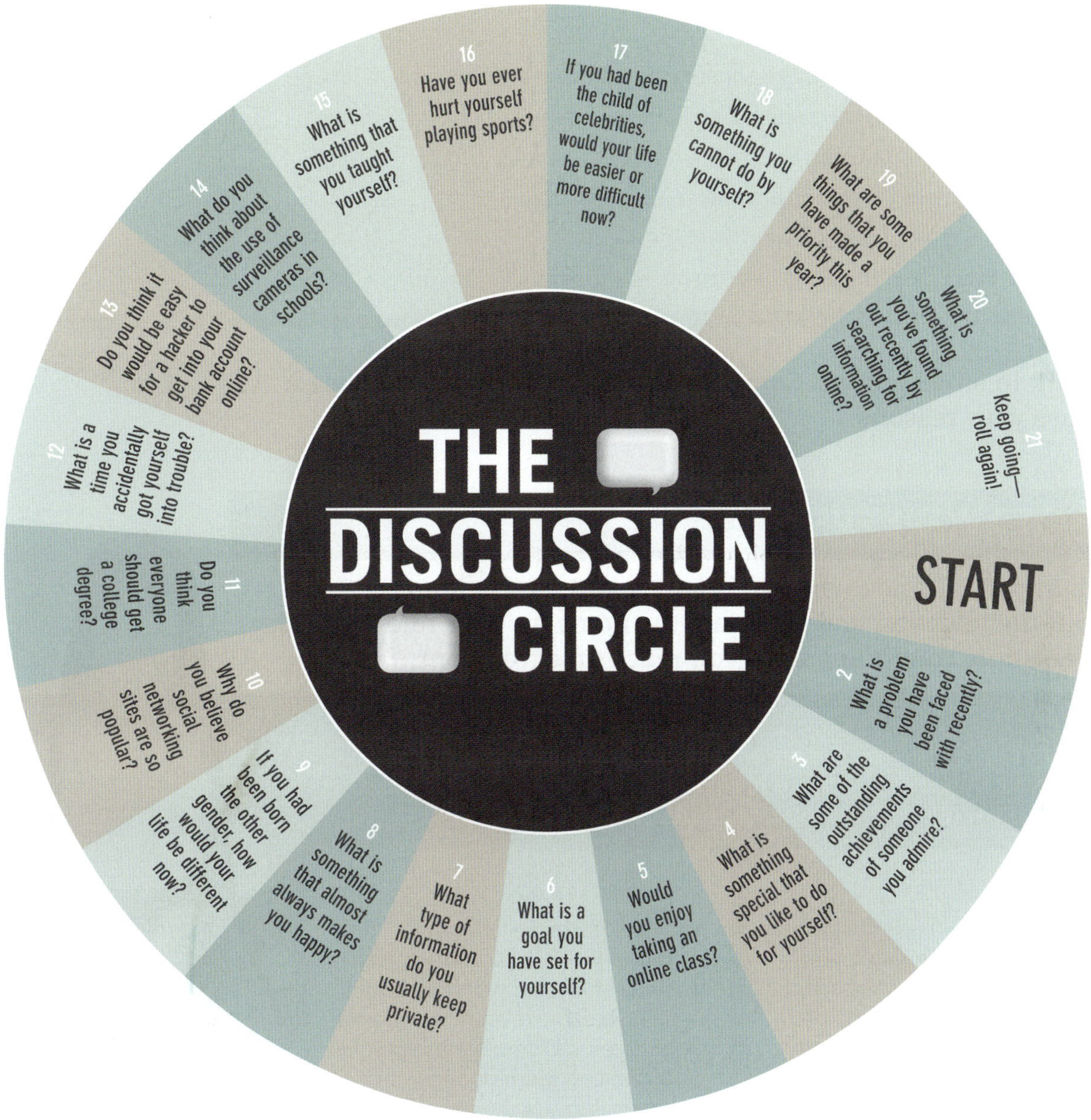

SCORE YOURSELF!

Score 1–5 for the items below. Score 5 for things that are easy and 1 for things that are difficult.

I can discuss issues related to internet crime.	5	4	3	2	1
I can talk about educational options and alternatives.	5	4	3	2	1
I can speculate on how past events have affected present situations.	5	4	3	2	1
I can participate effectively in group discussions.	5	4	3	2	1

If you gave yourself 1 or 2 for any of the statements, look at Units 3 and 4 again.

Communicative wrap-up
Units 5–6

1 21ST CENTURY LIVING

A Complete the survey about what you think life will be like in the middle of the 21st century.

BY 2050 ...		
robots will have been doing all domestic chores for several years.	Yes ☐	No ☐
animals will have been given the same basic rights as humans.	Yes ☐	No ☐
computers will have been thinking like people for over a decade.	Yes ☐	No ☐
zoos will have been made illegal and all wild animals set free.	Yes ☐	No ☐
we will have solved most of our environmental problems.	Yes ☐	No ☐
robots will have been given the same basic rights as humans.	Yes ☐	No ☐

B Work in small groups. Compare your answers from Exercise A and discuss your reasons.

2 ROBOT WORKERS

Work in pairs. Decide who is Student A and who is Student B. Then read about the situation and complete the notes for your role. Role-play the conversation, continuing until you reach an agreement.

The year is 2115. You are two people who own a small store. One of you (Student A) thinks you should buy a robot to replace one of your human workers. The other (Student B) feels unsure about the idea.

Student A:

You need to make Student B aware of the advantages. Find out what Student B is alarmed by and try to explain why there wouldn't be any problems. Complete the points and mention them during your conversation.

There's no need to be alarmed by robots because ________________.
Unlike human workers, robots are not distracted by ________________.
We'll be able to rely on a robot because ________________.

Student B:

You need to make Student A aware of the disadvantages. Find out why Student A wants a robot, and try to explain why there would be problems. Complete the points and mention them during your conversation.

Customers would be suspicious of a robot because ________________.
There are a number of risks, including ________________.
Another problem to be aware of is ________________.

3 EXOTIC PETS

A Work in pairs. Prepare for a debate about keeping exotic animals as pets. Your teacher will tell you whether to argue for or against the idea. List the points you want to make. These questions may help you.

- Should all animals be free to live in their natural habitat? Do all animals have basic rights?
- Does it depend on the kind of animal? Is it OK to keep some exotic animals as pets but not others?
- Is it wrong for anyone to keep exotic animals as pets, or could we have some kind of licensing system?
- Are there any benefits to endangered species from being kept as pets? Could it actually help the species in the wild in some way?

B With your partner, work with another pair that is taking the opposite position from you. Present your argument from Exercise A. The pair that is for keeping exotic animals as pets presents its argument first. Then the other pair replies with its counter-argument. Who do you think has the better case?

4 THE IDEAL DOMESTIC ROBOT

A Work in pairs. Design the ideal robot for the home. Decide what features it should have and what it should be able to do. Think about the needs of this family:

- Gordon and Claudia, the parents
- Cory, the 15-year-old son
- Melissa, the 7-year-old daughter

B Join another pair. With your partner, present your robot design. Explain how your robot meets the needs of the family and how it could be used to make their lives better.

SCORE YOURSELF!

Score 1–5 for the items below. Score 5 for things that are easy and 1 for things that are difficult.

I can speculate about future achievements.	5	4	3	2	1
I can adopt and present arguments from different points of view.	5	4	3	2	1
I can debate the idea of keeping exotic animals as pets.	5	4	3	2	1
I can discuss pros and cons and describe features of robots.	5	4	3	2	1

If you gave yourself 1 or 2 for any of the statements, look at Units 5 and 6 again.

Grammar reference

UNIT 1

ADVERB PHRASES

Function **Adverb phrases can be used to describe time, frequency, place, manner, and purpose. They answer the questions *when, how often, where, how,* and *why*.**

Type of adverb	Question answered	Adverb phrases	Example
Time	When	*last week, the next day,* etc.	*We went to the farmer's market* ***a few days ago.***
Frequency	How often	*every day, sometimes,* etc.	***From time to time,*** *I volunteer for a children's charity.*
Place	Where	Introduced by a preposition of place: *out of, in, on,* etc.	*We had a picnic lunch* ***under a shady tree.***
Manner	How	Introduced by *by*	*You can reduce your carbon footprint* ***by recycling waste.***
Purpose	Why	Introduced by *to, in order to, so as to*	***To find out more information,*** *visit our website.*

1 Match the underlined adverb phrases with the question words.

1 I walk to work <u>to keep in shape</u>.
2 I look <u>in the local newspaper</u> to find good second-hand cars.
3 I help local farmers <u>by not buying products from large supermarkets</u>.

a) Where
b) How
c) Why

2 Underline the adverb phrase in each sentence. Then write the type of adverb.

1 Let's get rid of these clothes by recycling them. ________
2 To save money, check when stores have special offers. ________
3 There are many bartering websites on the internet. ________

NEGATIVE QUESTIONS

Function **Negative questions can be used when we expect the answer to be either *yes* or *no*. They can also be used to express an opinion in a less forceful way, inviting the other person to agree.**

Form **Negative questions are formed with an auxiliary verb + *n't* + subject.**
Isn't it cold today?

1 Use the prompts and answers in parentheses to make negative questions.

1 better / send her an email? (Yes, it would.)
____

2 get / a signal / in here? (No, I can't. Let's go outside.)
____

3 see / photos on Facebook? (No. Were they really embarrassing?)
____

2 Read the situations in parentheses and write negative questions.

1 (You think Michael's cousins visited him last Saturday.)
"Hey, Michael, ____?"
2 (You think it's too late to go for a coffee this afternoon.)
"Thanks, Mark, but ____?"
3 (You're sure Ava has been to Mexico.)
"Ava, ____?"

UNIT 2

FUTURE PASSIVE

Form **The future passive is formed with *will/may/might/could* + *be* + past participle.**
The moon will be colonized. People could be sent there to work.

Function **We use the future passive when we don't know who will do something, when it's obvious or not important who will do something, and when we want to emphasize an action rather than who or what will do the action. We can use *by* to say who or what will do the action.**

1 Match the sentences with the reasons for using the future passive.

1 The accused may be found guilty today.
2 Two free tickets will be given away.
3 The minimum wage will be increased next year.

a) We don't know who will do the action.
b) It's obvious who will do the action.
c) We want to emphasize the action, not who or what will do it.

2 Complete the rewritten sentences in the future passive.

1 Somebody might announce the Oscar nominees later.
The Oscar nominees ______________________________.
2 The tennis final could decide a winner today, provided it doesn't rain.
A winner ______________________________.
3 Mark's brother will drop him off at 9 p.m.
Mark ______________________________.

CONDITIONAL CONJUNCTIONS

Form **conditional conjunction + clause (subject + verb)**

Conditional conjunction	Meaning	Examples
since	Because it is true that	*It is important to preserve traditions since they bring people together.*
provided that *as long as*	Only if	*Solar is an excellent renewable energy provided that a region receives a lot of sunlight.* *You will get used to living abroad as long as you learn the language.*
unless	Except if	*Unless you work from home, you'll work normal office hours.*
(just) in case	Because it is possible that	*I'll send you a text message (just) in case you don't have access to email.*

1 Choose the correct option.

1 Using a bicycle to get around is a good idea *as long as* / *unless* you feel safe.
2 They say that knowledge is power, *since* / *just in case* it allows you to gain advantages over others.
3 I would advise you to back up your files *provided that* / *just in case* your laptop ever crashes.

2 Complete the sentences with conditional conjunctions.

1 Users might abandon social networking sites ______________ companies do more to protect online privacy.
2 I often buy second-hand furniture ______________ it is in good condition.
3 Many celebrities are treated like royalty in the U.S.A. ______________ they don't have a royal family.

UNIT 3

OBJECT COMPLEMENTS

Form & Function **After some verbs, we can provide information about the object of a sentence using an object complement. The object complement may be an adjective or a noun. Some verbs take only an adjective, some take only a noun, and some can take either one. After verbs such as *see*, *know*, or *describe*, we often use *as*.**

Form	Examples
subject + verb + object + adjective	*Did you find the movie funny?* *The flowers made Mom really happy.*
subject + verb + object + noun	*Most websites consider a password a necessity.* *The newspapers are calling him a hero.*
subject + verb + object + *as* + noun / adjective	*Her boss would describe her as capable.* *They don't see it as a reason not to go.*

1 Put the words in the correct order to form sentences.

1 met / and I found / her / Jack's fiancée / I / very / pleasant / . ______
2 in the city / this hotel / the website / called / the best / . ______
3 as / creative / would describe / her teacher / her / . ______

2 Rewrite the sentences using the words in parentheses.

1 Rival politicians said the mayor was a criminal. (*call*) ______
2 Reports suggest that identity theft is a worrying trend. (*describe*) ______
3 You should regularly clean your bedroom. (*keep*) ______

NEGATIVE STRUCTURES WITH *THINK*, *SUPPOSE*, ETC.

Function **The negative form of verbs of opinion and supposition changes with different verbs.**

Verbs	Affirmative	Negative
think, believe, imagine, feel	*I think the plane arrives at 3:00.*	*I don't imagine anyone wants that.*
hope, *guess, suspect, assume*	*I guess we'll arrive there at 8:00.*	*I hope they don't lose my number.*
suppose, expect	*I expect he'll bring the dog.*	*I don't expect he'll bring the dog.* *I expect he won't bring the dog.*

Affirmative short answers

In affirmative short answers, we always use *so*: *Is Martina coming today? Yes, I think so.*

Negative short answers

Verbs	Form	Examples
think, believe, imagine	subject + negative verb + *so*	*I don't think so.*
hope, guess, suspect, assume	subject + verb + *not*	*I guess not.*
suppose, expect	subject + verb + *not* subject + negative verb + *so*	*I suppose not.* *I don't suppose so.*

1 I don't guess I would like the movie if it had a lot of special effects.
2 Do you think fewer people will use social networking sites in the future? No, I think not.
3 I feel it's not possible for me to continue working here.

2 Rewrite the sentences using the verbs in parentheses.

1 I don't want Ben to bring his new girlfriend to the wedding. (*hope*) ______
2 It's unlikely that they would hire a graduate without soft skills. (*think*) ______
3 I doubt people are happy all the time. (*imagine*) ______

UNIT 4

RELATIVE PRONOUNS WITH –*EVER*

Function ***Whatever, whenever, however, whoever,*** **and** ***wherever*** **are used to talk about an unknown/general thing, time, manner, person, or place.**

Pronouns	Examples
whatever	*You should study whatever you want, if it will improve your employment prospects.* *Whatever restaurant you choose, check that it has a vegetarian option.*
whoever	*Whoever arrives first can help with the drinks.*
whenever, however, wherever	*However you look at it, the internet has changed the way we interact forever.* *I don't doubt we'll have a great time wherever we go on vacation.*

1 Choose the correct option.

1 If you speak English, you'll be able to communicate *wherever* / *whenever* you go.
2 *Whoever* / *Whenever* spoke to you must have given you the wrong information.
3 *However* / *Whatever* way you look at it, our current way of living does not favor the environment.

2 Complete the text with –*ever* relative pronouns.

The great advantage of taking an online course is the freedom to study **(1)** ________ you want. This means you can study at 7 a.m. or 11 p.m., depending on your other commitments. I would encourage prospective virtual students to ensure **(2)** ________ course they choose offers discussion boards and professors who are regularly online to help and offer advice. **(3)** ________ you study, either in class or online, you need to put in the effort and be interested in your topic.

MIXED CONDITIONALS

Function	Examples	Form
A current or general situation with a past result	If I weren't on a diet, I would have had some of that chocolate dessert.	*If* clause in 2nd conditional, result clause in 3rd conditional: *If* + past simple, ... *would/could/may/might have* + past participle
A past event or situation with a present result	If I had taken an introductory class, I would have a better idea of what the advanced class involved.	*If* clause in 3rd conditional, result clause in 2nd conditional: *If* + past perfect, ... *would/could/may/might* + infinitive

1 Decide which mixed conditional each sentence refers to. Write A if it describes a current situation with a past result, or B if it describes a past event with a present result.

1 If I spoke better Spanish, I probably would have gone and lived somewhere in Latin America. ____
2 If the CEO hadn't quit when he did, it stands to reason the company would show better annual profits. ____
3 Rachael wouldn't have ended up a victim of identity theft if she did more to protect herself online. ____

2 Complete the sentences with the correct form of the verbs from the box.

crash have retire

1 If I ________ from my stressful job earlier, I guess I would be happier now.
2 My laptop ________ this morning if I had anti-virus software.
3 Suzie would have been more relaxed if she ________ an important interview later today.

UNIT 5

IMPERSONAL PASSIVE

Function **The impersonal passive is more formal and less common than the active. It is used with reporting and opinion verbs: *assume, say, believe, claim, consider, estimate, think, know, recommend, report,* and *understand.***

Form	Examples	Active version of examples
Impersonal passive 1: *It* + passive + *that* clause	*It is said that beauty ideals change depending on the culture.*	*People say that beauty ideals change depending on the culture.*
Impersonal passive 2: subject + passive + infinitive	*Beauty ideals are said to change depending on the culture.*	*Scientists believe that global warming is responsible for extreme weather.*

1 Complete the rewritten sentences with the impersonal passive 1 or 2.

1 Experts believe that sharing the same life goals is important in a long-term relationship.
It ________________ sharing the same life goals is important in a relationship.
2 We estimate that over 1,000 homes are destroyed by flooding every year.
Over 1,000 homes ________________ destroyed by flooding every year.
3 Visitors to the island report an increase in tourism.
Tourism on the island ________________ increasing.

2 Write impersonal passive sentences using the words and phrases provided.

1 it / claim / water therapy / help people / relax
____
2 it / say / the dragon / represent / control over water / in Chinese mythology
____
3 tap water / think / have the same benefits / as bottled water
____

PASSIVE MODALS

Modal	Form	Function	Examples
can, could, may, might, will, would	modal verb + *be* + past participle	We use these forms to talk about present and past ability or future possibility in the passive.	*Istanbul might (not) be accepted as host city for the Olympics in 2020.* *Flights and accommodations will be included in the price.*
must, ought to, should	modal verb + *be* + past participle	We use these forms to talk about necessity and advisability in the passive.	*More foreign languages ought to be taught at colleges.*
could, can't may, might, must	modal verb + *be* / *have been* + past participle	We use these forms to talk about deduction and speculation in the present or past.	*Some animal habitats must have been affected by the fire.*
should	modal verb + *have been* + past participle	We use this form to give criticism of something that happened in the past.	*Late applications should (not) have been accepted.*

1 Choose the correct option to complete the sentences.

1 There are so many journalists here. A press conference *must be* / *must have been* called.
2 Travelers *will* / *ought* be encouraged not to visit protected beaches.
3 Personal databases might *hack* / *be hacked* if users don't choose a strong password.

2 Complete the sentences with *might, must,* or *should* and any other words you need.

1 Steps to counter the effects of global warming ________________ taken earlier.
2 Ethan just called me, and he's still at the airport. His flight ________________ delayed.
3 I've heard that employees at the museum ________________ given free entry to the new exhibition.

UNIT 6

FUTURE PERFECT

Function **The future perfect is used to describe an event that will be completed by a specific time in the future.**

Active or Passive	Form	Example
Active	*will/won't* + *have* + past participle	*The real value of many salaries will have fallen by 15% by the end of the decade.*
Passive	*will/won't* + *have been* + past participle	*Students will have been given feedback on their exam by the end of the week.*

1 Choose the correct option to complete the sentences..

1 Computers *won't have* / *won't have been* replaced people in the labor market in 2100 since many jobs will require thinking skills.
2 People are encouraged to keep learning throughout life because some skills they learn at school *will have* / *will have been* become obsolete by the time they're 30.
3 It is hoped that many listeners will have *inspired* / *been inspired* to volunteer for the organization, thanks to the presentation.

2 Complete the sentences with the correct forms of the verbs in parentheses.

1 Some academics argue that in a few years many white-collar jobs ________. (*automate*)
2 It is estimated that up to 50% of the world's biodiversity ________ extinct by 2100. (*become*)
3 By midnight, whoever wins tonight's final ________ a record contract with a major label. (*offer*)

FUTURE PERFECT PROGRESSIVE

Function **The future perfect progressive is used to describe an action or situation happening for a period of time until a specific time in the future.**

Form	Example
will/won't + *have been* + *–ing* form	*By the time I'm 40, I will have been teaching for almost 20 years.*

1 Find and correct the mistake in each sentence.

1 When they retire, most graduates today won't be working in the same career all their lives.
2 I've finally got an interview next week. That's over a year I will have been waited.
3 Next year, I'll have be living here for four years.

2 Complete these sentences with the future perfect progressive form of the verb in parentheses.

1 I ________ with Emma for five years next week. (*go out*)
2 Tomorrow, it ________ for a whole week. (*snow*)
3 How long ________ by the time you finish your postgraduate degree? (*study*)

Irregular verbs

Infinitive	Past simple	Past participle
be	was/were	been
become	became	become
begin	began	begun
break	broke	broken
bring	brought	brought
build	built	built
buy	bought	bought
catch	caught	caught
choose	chose	chosen
come	came	come
cost	cost	cost
cut	cut	cut
do	did	done
draw	drew	drawn
drink	drank	drunk
drive	drove	driven
eat	ate	eaten
fall	fell	fallen
feed	fed	fed
feel	felt	felt
find	found	found
fly	flew	flown
get	got	got
give	gave	given
go	went	gone
grow	grew	grown
hang	hung	hung
have	had	had
hear	heard	heard
hit	hit	hit
hold	held	held
hurt	hurt	hurt
keep	kept	kept
know	knew	known
leave	left	left
let	let	let
lose	lost	lost
make	made	made
meet	met	met
pay	paid	paid
put	put	put
read	read	read
ride	rode	ridden
ring	rang	rung
rise	rose	risen
run	ran	run
say	said	said
see	saw	seen
sell	sold	sold
send	sent	sent
set	set	set
sing	sang	sung
sit	sat	sat
speak	spoke	spoken
stand	stood	stood
stick	stuck	stuck
take	took	taken
teach	taught	taught
tell	told	told
think	thought	thought
throw	threw	thrown
understand	understood	understood
wake	woke	woken
wear	wore	worn
win	won	won
write	wrote	written

Pronunciation symbols

Vowels

ɪ	did
e	bed, neck
æ	bad, hand
ɒ	box
ʌ	but, mother
ʊ	book, good
ə	banana, computer
iː	feed
ɑː	father
ɔː	tall
uː	boot, food, student
ɜː	shirt, birthday
eɪ	date, table
aɪ	cry, eye
ɔɪ	boy
əʊ	comb, post
aʊ	about, how
ʊə	tour
eə	their
ɪə	here, near

Consonants

p	park, happy
b	back, hobby
t	tea
d	die
k	came, kitchen, quarter
g	game, go
f	face, photographer
v	vegetable
θ	thing, maths
ð	then, that
s	city, summer
z	please, goes
ʃ	she, shop
ʒ	leisure
h	hot, who
tʃ	chicken, watch
dʒ	jacket, orange
m	men
n	sun, know
ŋ	sung, singer
w	week, white
r	rain, writer
l	light, long
j	yes, use, music

NOTES

NOTES

NOTES

NOTES

NOTES

Macmillan Education
4 Crinan Street
London N1 9XW
A division of Springer Nature Ltd

Companies and representatives throughout the world

ISBN 978-0-230-49419-0

Written by Mickey Rogers, Steve Taylor-Knowles and Dorothy E. Zemach.

This edition published 2015
First edition published 2010

Designed by emc design limited.
Illustrated by Chris Chalik (The Bright Group International) p31

Cover design by Tony Richardson, Wooden Ark Ltd.
Cover photograph courtesy of Getty Images/Anna Bryukhanova.

Picture research by Susannah Jayes.

The authors would like to thank the schools, teachers and students whose input has been invaluable in preparing this new edition. They would also like to thank the editorial and design teams at Macmillan for doing such a great job of organizing the material and bringing it to life.

The publishers would like to thank the following educators who reviewed materials and provided us with invaluable insight and feedback for the development of *masterMind* 2nd edition:

Isidro Almedarez, Deniz Atesok, Monica Delgadillo, Elaine Hodgson, Mark Lloyd, Rufus Vaughan-Spruce, Kristof van Houdt, Rob Duncan, James Conboy, Jonathan Danby, Fiona Craig, Martin Guilfoyle, Rodrigo Rosa.

The authors and publishers would like to thank the following for permission to reproduce material:

'A Free Life is Rich' by Katie Roche published in the Sunday Times, 28th October 2012. © Times Newspapers Limited, 2012. Reprinted by permission of the publisher. www.thesundaytimes.co.uk. Material adapted from 'How Star Trek Inspired an Innovation' by Paul Sloane. Originally published on www.destination-innovation.com. Reprinted with permission. Material from 'Don't Expect Robots to Do it all for you – or steal your jobs' by Fay Schopen published in the Times Online, 18th June 2013. © Times Newspapers Limited 2013. Reprinted by permission of the publisher. www.thesundaytimes.co.uk

The authors and publishers would like to thank the following for permission to reproduce their photographs:

Alamy/age footstock Spain, S.L pp60, 70, Alamy/Art Directors & TRIP p53, Alamy/AY Media AS p24(cm), Alamy/Stephen Barnes/Military p79(tr), Alamy/Blend Images p17(cr), Alamy/Bill Cheyrou p19, Alamy/Cultura Creative pp76(br), 79(tl), Alamy/Dex Image p64(tcr), Alamy/Norman Eggert p57(4), Alamy/Dennis Hallinan p37, Alamy/Jiri Hubatka p69(3), Alamy/Craig Joiner Photography p26, Alamy/Philip Lewis p15(tr), Alamy/MBI p9(4), Alamy/maximimages.com p15(cl), Alamy/Mimadeo p32, Alamy/Sergey Mironov p33(tr), Alamy/PHOVOIR p9(1), Alamy/Radius Images p46, Alamy/Stephen Roberts Photography p69(4), Alamy/Robert Satinforth p44, Alamy/Alexey Solodov p56, Alamy/Spaces Images p29, Alamy/UpperCut Image p17(tcr), Alamy/YAY Media AS p15(tl); **AIESEC** (visit www.aiesec.org to find your global opportunity) p52; Photograph courtesy of **Mark Boyle** p10; **Corbis**/Bettmann p154, Corbis/TOSHIYUKI AIZAWA/Reuters p69(6), Corbis/Theo Allofs p59, Corbis/ELOY ALONSO/Reuters p22(tr), Corbis/Arthur Baensch p56(cr), Corbis/145/Bill Boch/Ocean p81(cl), Corbis/Blaine Harrington III p20(cl), Corbis/Frank Krahmer p57(1), Corbis/KIM KYUNG-HOON/Reuters p69(2), Corbis/Lawrence Manning p157(tr), Corbis/Tim Parnell p9(3), Corbis/2/Ed Reschke/Ocean p63, Corbis/Denis Scott p28, Corbis/Strauss/Curtis p9(2), Corbis/Silke Woweries p38; **Getty Images**/333bracket.com p41(tl), Getty Images/Jack Ambrose p20(cr), Getty Images/BJI/Blue Jean Images p44(cr), Getty Images/Blend Images – Peter Dressel p61(cl), Getty Images/Mark Bowden p55(tr), Getty Images/Anatole Branch p68(cr), Getty Images/Burke/Triolo Productions p152(tl), Getty Images/Caiaimage/Paul Bradbury p45(3), Getty Images/Neale Clarke p68, Getty Images/Mark D Callanan p27, Getty Images/Johannes Compaan p57(cm), Getty Images/CORDIER Sylvain/hemis.fr p57(5), Getty Images/Reinhard Dirschel p57(3), Getty Images/Gamma-Keystone via Getty Images p45(2), Getty Images/Troels Graugaard p64(cr), Getty Images/Kidstock p45(1), Getty Images/kosmozoo p24(r & l), Getty Images/Leren Lu p47, Getty Images/Robert McGuoey p62, Getty Images/moodboard p76(cr), Getty Images/Terry Moore/Stocktrek Images p69(1), Getty Images/Dimitri Otis p34, Getty Images/ Javier Pierini p157(cr), Getty Images/Jan Erik Posth p55(tl), Getty Images/Martin Puddy p41(b), Getty Images/Monty Rakusen p71, Getty Images/Chris Rout p40, Getty Images/Chris Schmidt p13, Getty Images/Science and Society Picture Library p21, Getty Images/kristian sekulic p39, Getty Images/SM/AIUEO p72, Getty Images/Topical Press Agency p69 (5), Getty Images/Detlev van Ravenswaay p152(b), Getty Images/Thomas Vogel p73, Getty Images/Jerry Whaley p8, Getty Images/WALTER ZERLA p8 (br), Getty Images/Yellow Dog Productions p14; **Rex Features**/Aflo p156, Rex Features/c.Paramount/Everett pp22(cl), 23; **Science Photo Library**/ROBERT GENDLER p25; **Thinkstock**/anshu18 p58, Thinkstock/daboost p20(cmr), Thinkstock/Jeffrey Hamilton p50, Thinkstock/lofilolo p36, Thinkstock/Jirsak p33(tl), Thinkstock/Jupiterimages p61(bcl), Thinkstock/Matike p32, Thinkstock/monkeybusinessimages pp15(cr), 16, Thinkstock/stillwords p57(2), Thinkstock/Irina Tischenko p33(tm), Thinkstock/Wavebreakmedia Ltd p48, Thinkstock/Dezhi Wei p65.

Printed and bound in Poland.

2018
005